MAIDSTONE

CW00687083

08. MAR 07
29/3/07
26. SEP 07

10 FEB 09

17 OCT 2009

31 OCT 2009

- 9 FEB 2010

- 1 NOV 2010

1 6 NOV 2010

1 0 NOV 2011

- 4 MAY 2012

- 6 FEB 2014
14 Feb.
25 March 14
Apl
19 June

130ct
2015

3 JUL 2014

Books should be returned or renewed by the
last date stamped above

21-11-22

11/7/15

03/01/23

Awarded for excellence
to Arts & Libraries

Kent
County
Council

C 152339193

THE LAND

Books by V. SACKVILLE-WEST

—

THE LAND

BY

V. SACKVILLE WEST

with woodcuts by
GEORGE PLANK

and an introduction by
NIGEL NICOLSON

FRANCES LINCOLN

FRANCES LINCOLN LTD
4 Torriano Mews
Torriano Avenue
London NW5 2RZ
www.franceslincoln.com

First published by
WILLIAM HEINEMANN Ltd 1926

THE LAND
The Land: Copyright © Vita Sackville-West 1926
Introduction: Copyright © Nigel Nicolson 1989

All rights reserved.
No part of this publication may be reproduced, stored in a retrieval system,
or transmitted, in any form, or by any means, electronic, mechanical,
photocopying, recording or otherwise without either prior permission in
writing from the publisher or a licence permitting restricted copying. In the
United Kingdom such licences are issued by the Copyright Licensing Agency,
90 Tottenham Court Road, London W1T 4LP.

A CIP catalogue record for this book is available from the British Library.

First Frances Lincoln Edition 2004

ISBN 0 7112 2359 9

Printed in England

2 4 6 8 9 7 5 3 1

KENT ARTS & LIBRARIES	
C152339193	
Cypher	15.11.04
821	£11.99

To
D. W.

CONTENTS

INTRODUCTION
THE PASTORAL POETRY OF VITA SACKVILLE-WEST

Vita Sackville-West hoped above all to be remembered as a poet. She thought her novels *The Edwardians* and *All Passion Spent* too facile to deserve the acclaim they attracted, and would have despaired that today she should be known mainly as a gardener and a prose writer about gardens, much as she loved her own. She considered *The Land* and *The Garden* (the latter she rated second in quality, but wrongly) as her claim to an enduring place in literature.

Vita was not a 'modern' poet. She once confessed to her husband, Harold Nicolson, that her poetic gears would not mesh with Eliot's or Auden's: 'It is something left out of my make-up . . . I mean just lack of interest in what must always be *temporary* things', like politics or ephemeral experiences, which modern poets, she believed, often expressed in language unintelligible to the ordinary reader. Her two major poems deal in part with the humdrum occupations of farm and garden, but her theme is universal, evoking the rhythm of the four seasons as they repeat themselves endlessly like the heavenly bodies circling above – she was fascinated by astronomy – and impose a pattern on the lives of those who work on and with the soil.

Vita stated as precisely as she could the subtleties of what she observed and thought. Her meaning is immediately clear, and discloses to the reader what he would probably never put into words himself but recognises as true, like 'Water alone remains untouched by snow', which everyone knows, but how few notice. She took immense pains with her writing: both poems, each about 2,500 lines long, needed years to complete and polish. *The Land*, first conceived in 1921, was begun in 1923 and finished in 1926, and she started *The Garden* early in 1939 and finished it late in 1945, overlapping the Second War at each end. Her successive drafts, now in the Huntington Library, California, reveal how she would return again and again to a line or single word that displeased her, until she found the phrase which fitted the metre and expressed her intention exactly: 'Little sullen moons of mistletoe', or 'Brings him achievement with the truce of age'. There is a homely felicity in the rhythm of her lines. She varied the blank verse which she normally used by breaking from time to time into rhymed couplets, and sometimes lyrics (she used italics, too, to give them emphasis), where she became more playful or more reflective, as in her lovely lines on fritillaries or the 'Island' passage, the most famous in *The Land*, which anticipates *The Garden* by its eulogy of the flowers she loved most. Her poetry has a sobriety, a balance, a gentleness and unfaltering taste. It is old fashioned, though nobody complained of that, in the deep tradition of English nature poetry. These lines, for instance, about sheep in winter,

> With looks of dumb despair, then sad-dispersed,
> Dig for the withered herb through heaps of snow

could have been written by Vita Sackville-West. In fact they come from Thomson's *The Seasons*, written exactly two centuries before. I think she was influenced by him, not by Virgil's *Georgics* as was commonly supposed, for she knew no Latin and did not read them in translation until she was halfway through *The Land*.

Vita was determined not to sentimentalize the countryman or his unending combat with the soil. Nobody has felt more profoundly the beauty of her Kentish landscape, but her purpose was to explain the alternating conflict and collaboration between man and nature which created it, and her wonder that something so lovely as a garden or a field of corn could emerge from so much muck, toil, wastage and mutual malevolence. She looked Nature straight in the eye, reacting against the romanticism and prettiness of nineteenth-century poets and painters, and found the land spiteful. Her labourers are peasants, little removed from serfs, their lives brutal and their manners loutish, taciturn and grave. They are not people, like Hardy's rustics, so much as symbolic figures in a landscape, yet there is a dignity about their labour because it is harsh, honest, anonymous and shaped, like their tools, by centuries of experience. So much nobler, she thought, than townsmen's lives, who

> Meet together, talk, and grow most wise,
> But they have lost, in losing solitude,
> Something, – an inward grace, the seeing eyes,
> The power of being alone.

Some critics felt that Vita had drawn too stark, too anachronistic, a picture. Where were the farmworkers' moments of joy, of companionship and love, the pub, the Church, the festivals and the cricket field? Why does she mention women and children so seldom? Why cast such scorn upon social change, or the encroaching means of lightening their daily work – the tractor, the baler and the car? There are no benign middlemen in *The Land*, no shopkeeper, no parson and no squire. Life is terribly basic. Winter, because it is the cruellest season, is counted the most typical, and the vagrant, dying in the snow, its symbol. Even her own farmland is denied its fecundity: 'Only a bold man ploughs the Weald for corn', she asserts of land which, before me as I write these words, is green with burgeoning wheat, and the garden behind me spangled with her flowers.

But Vita was resolved to pare her poem to the bone, to rid it of all soppiness, to restore to her countryside its medieval primitiveness and virtue by a salutary douche of pain. She introduces words of archaic origin, like undern, lusk, shrammel, winsel, boggart, yeavy, shippon; phrases like 'Eild sheep, wethers, hoggs and barren yoes', or, 'That mobled blossom and that wimpled tree', not to tease the reader, but to bring him up short by an obsolete, Jabberwocky word, to roughen the line, to suggest Anglo-Saxon or Chaucerian roots, and if it is not always intelligible nor to be found in any dictionary, the sense can be guessed from its onomatopoeic sound or deduced from the context, as if reading a foreign language with which one is not perfectly familiar.

There is another element in *The Land* which is rarely repeated in *The Garden*: its detailed instructions on how to govern the soil. Vita was not herself a farmer, but she owned a farm close to Long Barn, her house in the Weald of Kent, and let it to Vera Cardinal, whom she often visited and watched at work. Some of her most apt descriptions, like her clipped sheep which 'Staggers astonished from such curt release', or horses, 'Their shining shoes strike fire on errant flints', emerged from her close observation. Season by season she went down to the farm to watch a particular process and return home to turn it into words. I often accompanied her on such trips and, though she did not take notes, I would see her go straight to her study and tell me she was not to be disturbed. I was eight years old at the time.

Thus she moulded her didactic passages – how to build a hayrick, how to tend bees, reap corn, dry hops – supplementing her own observations by reference to a four-volume Encyclopaedia of Agriculture which Harold gave her, and farmers said they could not fault her. The swarming detail has a cumulative effect. The poem must be long to permit its full development, to suggest the slow turning of the seasons with their interpenetrating tasks and moods, and to contrast the mortality of man with self-renewing nature, a theme to which she returned with increasing anguish in *The Garden*.

She finished *The Land* in Persia, and dated it at the end, 'Isfahan, April 1926', which led some people to imagine that it was all written there. In fact, at Isfahan she added only the last twenty-four lines in proof, her invocation of Virgil whom she at last recognised as her progenitor.

O Mantuan! that sang the bees and vines,
The tillage and the flocks.

It is her most sublime passage, lifting her homesick love of England from the deepest wells of her memory. She was pleased with it, but many years later, in her own copy, she altered the penultimate line from 'Thou took'st the waxen tablets in thy hand' to 'You took the waxen tablets in your hand', thinking the first version too emollient and wishing to end her poem as austerely as she had begun.

The Land was awarded the Hawthornden Prize, and John Drinkwater, in presenting it to her, said that the poem contained some of the loveliest verse written that century. Most critics endorsed his praise: only Edith Sitwell voiced strong objections, calling it 'poetry in gumboots', which would 'be of great use to prospective farmers, for it is one long catalogue of agricultural omplements'. She cannot have read it. Virginia Woolf, who was always Vita's frankest critic, encouraged her to write another long poem, about a village. Vita began it immediately, but it was not about a village: it was *The Garden*. She told Harold, 'It will have much more in it than mere gardening – all my beliefs and unbeliefs'.

Vita put *The Garden* aside for many years while she was writing her best-known novels, then *Saint Joan of Arc*, *Pepita* and *The Eagle and the Dove*, and took it up again in February 1939, working on it intermittently throughout the war, of which she had a more direct experience than most of her countrywomen. Her two sons were serving in Africa and Italy, and her house, now Sissinghurst, lay immediately below the air-battles of 1940 and close to the front line of the expected German invasion. Once, a huge bomber, crashing in flames, missed her tower by a few feet. She was courageous and defiant, her innate conservatism matching her profound patriotism, and she found beauty in the grimmest manifestations of war, lake the searchlights,

> Slow scissors walking up and down the black,
> Soundless collision of their closing blades,

or a bird struck dead by a bomb falling in her own fields, on which she wrote one of her loveliest lyrics, 'It took a ton of iron to kill this lark'.

To her, the garden was a luxury in war ('Small pleasures must correct great tragedies'), and though it was perforce neglected and its lawns became hayfields, her plants continued to blossom unaware of the human crisis. Vita had a fellow-feeling for her flowers. For her they had almost personal characteristics, exuberance and sulkiness, arrogance and modesty, and she never lost her astonishment that something so short-lived, with no middle-age between bud and death, could put itself to so much trouble to look so beautiful. Her long passage about tulips is one example, and another, on daffodils and narcissus, expresses her amazement that a blade so tender and flexible could thrust its way upwards with such determination. Nature does most, she insisted, the gardener least.

Vita describes in detail how to cut hedges or to pot and prune, but now her purpose is more meditative, *The Garden* is profounder poem than *The Land*. The notes she addressed to herself on the margins of her manuscript reveal her main concerns: 'Courage in adversity: Determination to find pleasure and not succumb'; 'Dislike of modern life and vulgarity; love of the graces of life and retirement'. She felt a spiritual weariness, regretted her advancing age (though she was only forty-eight in 1940), remembered with a sigh the daring of her youth, and foresaw the end of life, rising in despair to capital letters:

ONE HOUR WILL BE THE HOUR OF DEATH . . .
IT IS ALREADY LATER THAN YOU THINK.

Vita was not formally religious, but she had pondered deeply, when writing *The Eagle and the Dove*, on religion's mysteries, and wished herself more receptive to its consolations. Her mood was sombre, her meditations suffused with melancholy, from which she aroused herself by examining the perfection of a flower.

On the day before publication in 1946 she hid herself in a wood 'from sheer misery' as she wrote in her diary, 'failing as gardener, failing as poet', as she wrote in the poem itself. She need not have worried. *The Garden* was widely acclaimed and won another prize, the Heinemann. Together, the two poems can stand as the testimony of a writer who won from the soil the tribute she gave it.

Nigel Nicolson
Sissinghurst Castle, Kent

THE LAND

Nec sum animi dubius, verbis ea vincere magnum
quam sit et angustis hunc addere rebus honorem.

Georgics, Book III, 289–90

WINTER

WINTER

I SING the cycle of my country's year,
  I sing the tillage, and the reaping sing,
Classic monotony, that modes and wars
Leave undisturbed, unbettered, for their best
Was born immediate, of expediency.
The sickle sought no art; the axe, the share
Draped no superfluous beauty round their steel;
The scythe desired no music for her stroke,
Her stroke sufficed in music, as her blade
Laid low the swathes; the scythesmen swept, nor cared
What crop had ripened, whether oats in Greece
Or oats in Kent; the shepherd on the ridge
Like his Boeotian forebear kept his flocks,
And still their outlines on our tenderer sky
Simple and classic rear their grave design
As once at Thebes, as once in Lombardy.

I sing once more
The mild continuous epic of the soil,
Haysel and harvest, tilth and husbandry;
I tell of marl and dung, and of the means

That break the unkindly spirit of the clay;
I tell the things I know, the things I knew
Before I knew them, immemorially;
And as the fieldsman of unhurrying tread
Trudges with steady and unchanging gait,
Being born to clays that in the winter hold,
So my pedestrian measure gravely plods,
Telling a loutish life. I have refused
The easier uses of made poetry,
But no small ploy disdain to chronicle,
And (like that pious yeoman laid to rest
Beneath the legend that told all his life
In five hard words: "He tilled the soil well")
Prune my ambition to the lowly prayer
That I may drive the furrow of my tale
Straight, through the lives and dignities I know.

Why should a poet pray thus? poets scorn
The boundaried love of country, being free
Of winds, and alien lands, and distances,
Vagabonds of the compass, wayfarers,
Pilgrims of thought, the tongues of Pentecost
Their privilege, and in their peddler's pack
The curious treasures of their stock-in-trade,
Bossy and singular, the heritage
Of poetry and science, polished bright,
Thin with the rubbing of too many hands:
Myth, glamour, hazard, fables dim as age,

4

Faith, doubt, perplexity, grief, hope, despair,
Wings, and great waters, and Promethean fire,
Man's hand to clasp, and Helen's mouth to kiss.
Why then in little meadows hedge about
A poet's pasture? shed a poet's cloak
For fustian? cede a birthright, thus to map
So small a corner of so great a world?

The country habit has me by the heart.
He is bewitched forever who has seen,
Not with his eyes but with his vision, Spring
Flow down the woods and stipple leaves with sun,
As each man knows the life that fits him best,
The shape it makes in his soul, the tune, the tone,
And after ranging on a tentative flight
Stoops like the merlin to the constant lure.
The country habit has me by the heart;
I never hear the sheep-bells in the fold,
Nor see the ungainly heron rise and flap
Over the marsh, nor hear the asprous corn
Clash, as the reapers set the sheaves in shocks
(That like a tented army dream away
The night beneath the moon in silvered fields),
Nor watch the stubborn team of horse and man
Graven upon the skyline, nor regain
The sign-posts on the roads towards my home
Bearing familiar names—without a strong
Leaping of recognition; only here

Lies peace beyond uneasy truancy;
Here meet and marry many harmonies,
—All harmonies being ultimately one,—
Small mirroring majestic; for as earth
Rolls on her journey, so her little fields
Ripen or sleep, and the necessities
Of seasons match the planetary law.
So truly stride between the earth and heaven
Sowers of grain: so truly in the spring
Earth's orbit swings both blood and sap to rhythm,
And infinite and humble are at one;
So the brown hedger, through the evening lanes
Homeward returning, sees above the ricks,
Sickle in hand, the sickle in the sky.

Shepherds and stars are quiet with the hills.
There is a bond between the men who go
From youth about the business of the earth,
And the earth they serve, their cradle and their grave.
Stars with the season alter; only he
Who wakeful follows the pricked revolving sky,
Turns concordant with the earth while others sleep;
To him the dawn is punctual; to him
The quarters of the year no empty name.
A loutish life, but in the midst of dark
Cut to a gash of beauty, as when the hawk
Bears upwards in its talons the striking snake,
High, and yet higher, till those two hang close,

6

Sculptural on the blue, together twined,
Exalted, deathly, silent, and alone.

And since to live men labour, only knowing
Life's little lantern between dark and dark,
The fieldsman in his grave humility
Goes about his centennial concerns,
Bread for his race and fodder for his kine,
Mating and breeding, since he only knows
The life he sees, how it may best endure,
(But on his Sabbath pacifies his God,
Blindly, though storm may wreck his urgent crops,)
And sees no beauty in his horny life,
With closer wisdom than soft poets use.
But I, like him, who strive
Closely with earth, and know her grudging mind,
Will sing no songs of bounty, for I see
Only the battle between man and earth,
The sweat, the weariness, the care, the balk;
See earth the slave and tyrant, mutinous,
Turning upon her tyrant and her slave,
Yielding reluctantly her fruits, to none
But most peremptory wooers.
Wherever waste eludes man's vigilance,
There spring the weeds and darnels; where he treads
Through woods a tangle nets and trips his steps;
His hands alone force fruitfulness and tilth;
Strange lovers, man and earth! their love and hate

7

Braided in mutual need; and of their strife
A tired contentment born.

I then, who as a wrestler wrought with earth
Bending some stubborn acres to my will,
Know that no miracle shall come to pass
Informing man, no whisper from Demeter,—
Miraculous strength, initiated lore.
Nothing but toil shall serve him; in their rote
The seasons shall compel his constancy,
(The fields not always fair, nor prospects kind,)
Year ripen year, and timely foresight yield
Its measure in due course. And so I sing
Without illusion, seeing fieldsmen go
Heads lowered against sleet, hands frozen red,
Without complaint, but only patient, patient:
So in December sing I, while they come
Weary and dull and silent, tramping home
Through rainy dark, the cowman taking down
The hurricane lantern from its usual peg,
And going round the cattle in the stalls,
The shifting, munching cattle in the dark
And aromatic stalls beneath the rafters,
Swinging the lantern as he goes his rounds.
Clapping the kine upon their bony rumps
And seeing to their comfort ere he comes
Back to the ruddy kitchen for his food,
—Thus sing in winter, watching by the fire:

Many have sung the summer's songs,
Many have sung the corn,
Many have sung white blossom too
That stars the naked thorn—
That stars the black and naked thorn
Against the chalky blue.

But I, crouched up beside the hearth,
Will sing the red and gray;
Red going-down of sun behind
Clubbed woods of winter's day;
Of winter's short and hodden day
That seals the sober hind:

Seals him sagacious through the year
Since winter comes again;
Since harvest's but another toil
And sorrow through the grain
Mounts up, through swathes of ripest grain
The sorrow of the soil.

No lightness is there at their heart,
No joy in country folk;
Only a patience slow and grave
Beneath their labour's yoke,—
Beneath the earth's compelling yoke
That only serves its slave,

9

Winter
Song

Since countryman forever holds
The winter's memory,
When he, before the planets' fires
Have faded from the sky,
From black, resplendent winter sky
Must go about his byres;

And whether to the reaper's whirr
That scythes the falling crops,
He travels round the widening wake
Between the corn and copse,
The stubble wake 'twixt corn and copse
Where gleaners ply the rake,

Or whether in his granary loft
He pours the winnowed sacks,
Or whether in his yard he routs
The vermin from the stacks,
The vermin from the staddled stacks
With staves and stones and shouts,

Still, still through all the molten eves
Whether he reaps or hones,
Or counts the guerdon of his sweat,
Still to his inward bones,
His ancient, sage, sardonic bones,
The winter haunts him yet.

Winter and toil reward him still　　　　　*Winter*
While he his course shall go　　　　　　　*Song*
According to his proven worth,
Until his faith shall know
The ultimate justice, and the slow
Compassion of the earth.

Hear first of the country that shall claim my theme,　*An-*
The Weald of Kent, once forest, and to-day　　　　*dreds-*
Meadow and orchard, garden of fruit and hops,　　*weald*
A green, wet country on a bed of clay,
From Edenbridge to Appledore and Lympne
Drained by the Medway and the Rother stream,
With forest oaks still hearty in the copse,
For this was Sylva Anderida. Here
Stretched Andredsweald, and joined the wood of Blean,
Forest and warren, cropped by herds of deer,
And droves of swine that stirred the oak-trees' mast,
So wild a tract, so darkly green,
No stranger might forsake the trodden way,
Or venture through the trees towards the dene,
But on his horn must blow a warning blast;
No stranger, under Ina's law, might burn the tree,
And send the flame to sear the leaf;
If so he did, he must pay grudgingly
The fullest fine, for fire's a silent thief;
But if he took an axe to fell the oak,

An-
dreds-
weald

Even several oaks, as many as might be,
Then must he pay for three, not more than three,
For axe is an informer, not a thief,
And at the felling loud in protest spoke.

This was the Weald, compact of forest laws,
Pannage and Gavelswine, Danger and Corredy;
Unhandseled, separate, dark;
Where herdsman, seeking through the sunless days
For berry and for nut,
Shaggy with skins and hung with scarlet haws,
While hogs between the trees went grunting ways,
Lived a brute's life with brutes, and scored the bark
To blaze the track that led him to his hut.
This was the Weald, but as man conquers slow
Each province of his fief,—poor simple land
Or ravelled knowledge,—so the tardy herd,
Waking to action, by impatience stirred,
Bethought him he might throw
Trees round his hovel, clearings make by hand,
And in the sunlight let his children go.

So grew the dene.
Next came the wooden plough,
Turning the furrows of the first bold field,
A patch of light, a square of paler green,
Cupped in the darkness of the Weald.
Hedges fenced off the boar, the bundling sow

Followed by squealing litter; hedges made
By loppings of the bough,
With teinage rudely thrust between.

*An-
dreds-
weald*

Thus the foundations of the farm were laid.

The common saying goes, that on the hill
A man may lie in bed to work his farm,
Propping his elbows on his window-sill
To watch his harvest growing like a charm.
But the man who works the wet and weeping soil
Down in the Weald, must marl and delve and till
His three-horse land, fearing nor sweat nor droil.
For through the winter he must fight the flood,
The clay, that yellow enemy, that rots
His land, sucks at his horses' hooves
So that his waggon plunges in the mud,
And horses strain, but waggon never moves;
Delays his plough, and holds his spud
With yeavy spite in trenching garden-plots;
The catchy clay, that does its utmost harm,
And comes into his house, to spoil
Even his dwelling, creeps into his bones
Before their time, and makes them ache,
Leaving its token in his husky tones;
And all through summer he must see the clay
Harden as brick, and bake,

*The
Weald
of Kent*

13

The And open cracks to swallow up his arm,
Weald Where neither harrow, hoe, nor rake
of Kent Can rasp a tilth, but young and eager shoots
Pierce into blank, and wither at the roots.
Yet with his stupid loyalty he will say,
Being a wealden man of wealden land,
Holding his wealden honour as a pledge,
"In times of drought those farms up on the ridge,
Light soil, half sand,
With the first summer gale blow half away,"
And lifts his eyes towards the hill with scorn.

But only a bold man ploughs the Weald for corn,
Most are content with fruit or pasture, knowing
Too well both drought and winter's heavy going;
So the lush Weald to-day
Lies green in distance, and the horizon's sweep
Deepens to blue in woods, with the pointed spire
Pricking the foreground by the village tiles,
And the hop-kiln's whitened chimney stares between
Paler and darker green of Kentish miles,
And rarely a patch of corn in metal fire
Burnished by sunset ruffles in the green;
But meadow, shaw, and orchard keep
The glaucous country like a hilly sea
Pure in its monotone. Sad eyes that tire
Of dangerous landscape, sadder minds
That search impossible regions of their quest,

14

Find clement haven after truancy,

The

A temperate answer, and a makeshift rest.

Weald

This is the thing familiar, known;

of Kent

The safety that the wanderer finds,
Out of the world, one thing his own.
A pause, a lull in journeying, return
After the querying and astonishment;
Reward that only rovers earn
Who have strayed, departed from the peace,
Whether in soul or body widely flown,
Gone after Arabian Nights, the Golden Fleece,
And come back empty-handed, as they went.

Hear next of winter, when the florid summer,

Winter

The bright barbarian scarfed in a swathe of flowers,
The corn a golden ear-ring on her cheek,
Has left our north to winter's finer etching,
To raw-boned winter, when the sun
Slinks in a narrow and a furtive arc,
Red as the harvest moon, from east to west,
And the swans go home at dusk to the leaden lake
Dark in the plains of snow.

Water alone remains untouched by snow.

Here is no colour, here but form and structure,
The bones of trees, the magpie bark of birches,

Winter   Apse of trees and tracery of network,
Fields of snow and tranquil trees in snow
Through veils of twilight, northern, still, and sad,
Waiting for night, and for the moon
Riding the sky and turning snow to beauty,
Pale in herself as winter's very genius,
Casting the shadows delicate of trees,
Moon-shadows on the moon-lit snow, the ghost
Of shadows, veering with the moving moon,
Faint as the markings on the silver coin
Risen in heaven,—shades of barren ranges,
Craters, and lunar Apennines, and plains
Old as the earth, and cold as space, and empty,
Whence Earth appears a planet far surpassing
Our ken of any star for neighbouring splendour,
Her continents, her seas, her mountain ranges
Splendid and visible, majestic planet
Sweeping through space, and bearing in her train
Her silver satellite that sees no strife,
No warring of her men, no grief, no anger,
No blood spilt red to stain the golden planet,
But sees her architecture royally:
Dark Asia; islands; spread of the Pacific;
The silver satellite that casts the ghost
Of ghostly trees across the fields of snow.

Now in the radiant night no men are stirring:
The little houses sleep with shuttered panes;

Only the hares are wakeful, loosely loping *Winter*
Along the hedges with their easy gait,
And big loose ears, and pad-prints crossing snow;
The ricks and trees stand silent in the moon,
Loaded with snow, and tiny drifts from branches
Slip to the ground in woods with sliding sigh.
Private the woods, enjoying a secret beauty.

But one man comes, one outcast and a vagrant *Vagrant*
Having no roof to keep him from the snow;
Comes with a shuffling step between the trees;
Vague, old; and sinks upon a fallen bole,
Merging himself in night till silence gains him,
And hares play fearless round him in the shadows
Cast by the moon. Whence comes he? what have been
His annals? what but annals of long roads,
All roads alike, made sharp by hostile eyes,
—Rightly, he yields it, in his resignation,—
Whence has he shambled, into snow-bound Kent?
Out of what night of lassitude and despair
Into this night of beauty and cold death?
What sire begot, what mother cradled him?
He drowses on his bole, while snow-flakes gather,
While snow-flakes drift and gather,
Touching his darkness with their white, until
He grows to an idol in the wood forgotten,
Image of what men were, to silence frozen,
Image of contemplation and enigma,

17

Vagrant   So stiffens in his death. His old coat covers
His heart's vain hieroglyph. But still the hares
Play hopscotch with the shadows, having less fear
Of death's quiescence than of life's quick danger,
In a world where men are truant, night to dawn,
Suspended hours when life's poor common business
Lies dormant in a world to silence given,
Given to silence and the slanting moon.

Shep-   Only the shepherd watching by his flock
herd   Sees the moon wax and wane; endures the time
When frost is sharpest; hears the steeple chime
Each hour neglected; hears the rutting brock
Scream in the night; the prowling dog-fox bark;
Snared rabbit cry, small tragedy of dark.

The shepherd watching by his ewes and theaves
All night in loneliness, each cry knows well,
Whether the early lambing on the Downs
Rob him of Christmas, or on slopes of fell
March keep him crouching, shawled against the sleet;
But there's a cry that drowns
All else to shepherd's ears: the wavering bleat
Of weakling newly-born: then he shall lift
The lanky baby to his own warm hut,
Lay it on straw, and shift
Closer the lamp, and set the bottle's teat

18

With good warm milk between the lips half-shut,   *Shep-*
Coaxing the doubtful life, while wind and rain   *herd*
Against the window of the cabin beat,
And homing cottars in the plain below
Look up, and seeing the window's yellow glow,
Mutter, "The shepherd's at his job again."

Poor heavy-sided ewes must have their care;
Pasture, and in their pens a bite of hay.
Poor roots, good lambs; good roots, poor lambs, they say;
So shall the prudent shepherd keep them spare,
And likewise short of cake before they ean;
And he shall set the double hurdles square
Against the north and east with straw between,
For shelter; he shall run his ewes and lambs
In various pens: the twins, the little rams,
And frolic younglings just about to wean;
He shall turn little rams to little tegs,
And dock their tails, but on a different day;
Then, well content, sit down to watch them play,
Companioned by his pipe and towsled pup;
Watch them, appraising strong and frisky legs,
And grin when little ewe butts little tup.

But while the shepherd lonely in his cotes   *Yeoman*
Lives the harsh months decreed,
The farmer, thwarted by the early dusk,
Uses the hours that keep his ploughman lusk,

Yeoman   And plans his year for pasture or for seed.
Champion and several each claim their meed;
Fallow, and arable, and clover ley;
Shall the Ten-Acre carry sheep or oats?
Shall the poor Roughets stand this year for hay?

For now when fields beneath the wintry light
Lie stark, and snow along the hedgerow clings,
When streams of rooks on swerving wings
Blacken the sky with their untidy flight,
When iron ridges bind the frozen clay,
And sunset reddens cart-ruts on the road,—
Now in the wolf-month, shrammed and gaunt,
When vixens prowl, and hopping birds grow bold,
And craven otters haunt
The coops, by famine driven, and by cold,—
There's little chance for labour on the land.
Only the dung-cart with its reasty load
Creaks safe across the fields on frozen ground,
And horses for the fork or shovel stand
Patient, their nostrils smoking on the air.
Carting's a winter job. The strawy mound,
The wedge-shaped hale of roots for winter feeding
        stored,
Gapes, and gives up its rolling, orange hoard,
Cut in the farmyard troughs to equal share.
There's little else in these dead months to keep
The farm-folks brisk; at dawn and dusk they go

To break the ice on inky water-holes;   *Yeoman*
Fold on fresh patch of swedes the fattening sheep;
Put in a casual hour to dig out moles.
All desultory tasks, while the short day
Dulls from the morning's red to undern grey,
And dyes to red again as sun sinks low.

Pencil in hand beneath the hanging lamp
The farmer ponders in the kitchen's hush;
In the dark shippon tranquil cattle crush
Sweet cake, sliced mangold; shift, and blow, and champ;
In the dark stable tired horses stamp,
And nuzzle at the manger for their feed.
But though the homestead in such quiet doze
Under the double spell of night and frost,
Within the yeoman's kitchen scheme
The year revolves its immemorial prose.
He reckons labour, reckons too the cost;
Mates up his beasts, and sees his calf-run teem;
Takes pigs to market underneath a net;
Sees blossom on his orchards in the spring;
Sees rows of roots, all plump and stoutly set,
And hears the windy barley hiss
Like golden snakes before good harvesting;
And, since no little winsel comes amiss,
Cozens the dullards that go marketing.

He'd cheat a fool indeed, but do no worse;

Yeoman　　His heart is wider than his purse,
Take all in all; but narrower than each
The portals of his speech.
Few words must serve his turn,
For he's sagacious who lives taciturn,
And airs no noisy cunning of his trade,
But keeps his private purpose deeply laid;
Gives neighbours nothing of his confidence,
And takes his counsel of his own good sense.
No wise man utters what he inly knows;
Certainty in a loose uncertain world
Is far too firm a treasure; wiseman goes
Jealous and wary, keeping darkly furled
His small particular knowledge. So he plots
To get the better of his lands again;
Compels, coerces, sets in trim, allots,
Renews the old campaign.
His mind is but the map of his estate,
No broader than his acres, fenced and bound
Within the little England of his ground,
Squared neat between the hedgerows of his brain,
With here Lord's Meadow tilted on a hill,
And Scallops' Coppice ending in a gate,
And here the Eden passing by a mill,
And there the barn with thatch,
And here a patch of gorse, and there a patch
Of iris on the fringes of a pond,
And here Brook Orchard banded safe with grease;

All this he sees, and nothing sees beyond   *Yeoman*
The limits and the fealty of his lease.
Tenant of his inheritance,
Brief link in life's long circumstance,
One of the nameless, name-forgotten line
Descended from that nameless ancestor
Who cut a holding in the serried weald
Where droves of swine
Rootled for acorns underneath the oaks,
Anderida's sole yield
When Drake played bowls at Plymouth, and the rare
Coach with the cumbrous spokes
Trundled along the single clay-wet track
To Sussex with drawn blinds, or journeyed back
To London on affairs of state, the fine
Heraldic blazon eloquent on the door;
Makers of land, one of the nameless line
That fenced, and tilled, and overcame the waste,
And cut the necessary gaps,
And shaped the fields, slow-paced,
Into their permanent design,
Each field with local name, not marked on maps,
How come by, how begotten,
Long since forgotten:
Clement's, the Roundabout, Black Mead and Bitter
      Docks,
Rough Shepherd, Horses' Houghs,
And trod the path that grew into this lane

23

Yeoman   Bending between the hedgerows, where
              Convenience claimed a road,—for country road
              Is natural growth, with here a curve
              Skirting a tree felled long ago, a swerve
              To let the rattling harrow pass, the wain
              With trussed and swaying load
              Lurch safely by, and empty pass again.

              He tills the soil to-day,
              Surly and grave, his difficult wage to earn.
              Cities of discontent, the sickened nerve,
              Are still a fashion that he will not learn.
              His way is still the obstinate old way,
              Even though his horses stare above the hedge,
              And whinny, while the tractor drives its wedge
              Where they were wont to serve,
              And iron robs them of their privilege.
              Still is his heart not given
              To such encroachments on a natural creed;
              Not wholly given, though he bows to need
              By urgency and competition driven,
              And vanity, to follow with the tide.
              Still with a secret triumph he will say,
              "Tractor for sand, maybe, but horse for clay,"
              And in his calling takes a stubborn pride
              That nature still defeats
              The frowsty science of the cloistered men,
              Their theory, their conceits;

24

The faith within him still derides the pen,   *Yeoman*
Experience his text-book. What have they,
The bookish townsmen in their dry retreats,
Known of December dawns, before the sun
Reddened the east, and fields were wet and grey?
When have they gone, another day begun,
By tracks into a quagmire trodden,
With sacks about their shoulders and the damp
Soaking until their very souls were sodden,
To help a sick beast, by a flickering lamp,
With rough words and kind hands?
Or felt their boots so heavy and so swere
With trudging over cledgy lands,
Held fast by earth, being to earth so near?

Book-learning they have known.
They meet together, talk, and grow most wise,
But they have lost, in losing solitude,
Something,—an inward grace, the seeing eyes,
The power of being alone;
The power of being alone with earth and skies,
Of going about a task with quietude,
Aware at once of earth's surrounding mood
And of an insect crawling on a stone.

SPRING

SPRING

THE peddler and the reddleman
   Go vagrant through the shires.
The peddler tempts the farmer's wife
With all she most admires,
With beads, and boxes made of shells,
With lace and huckaback,
Buckles for shoes and rings for ears,
And Old Moore's Almanack,
With tapes and bobbins, pins and thread,
"What lack you? what d'you lack?"

The reddleman from head to foot
Dyed in his scarlet dye,
Leans like the Devil on the gate,
And grins when children cry.
"Redd for your sheep today, shepherd?
Redd for your yoes and rams?
I never broke a tup's leg yet
Or scared the mothering dams.
You'll find me natty at my job,
And gentle with the lambs."

Fra-
ternity

Fra-
ternity

The tinker and the boggart both
Long since have learnt by rote
How cold the rain and sharp the wind
Drive through a ragged coat.
The tinker with his little cart
Hawking his tinny wares,
Puts down his head against the sleet
And whimpers for repairs.
"Kind lady, patch your pots and pans,
And mend your broken chairs?"

The boggart on the frosty ridge,
His sleeveless arms held wide,
Stands gaunt against the wintry sky
Forever crucified.
A raven perched upon his hat,
About his feet the crows,
How bleak December turns the fields,
How desolate the snows,
How long the nights and short the days,
Tatterdemalion knows.

Spring

There's no beginning to the farmer's year,
Only recurrent patterns on a scroll
Unwinding; only use in step with need,
Sharp on the minute when the minute's come;
A watching, waiting thole,

A reckoning by rule-of-thumb.   *Spring*
You may see wealden farmers plough for seed
Before July is out, or dung and drudge
Midsummer yet being here,
Using the drought to carry horse and wain,
Else sinks the hoof to the fetlock, axles strain,
Tines choke. Let farmers do as farmers judge.

Therefore let no man say, "Peas shall be sown
This month or that; now shall the harrow go;
Now scuffle with deep coulters, now with shallow;
Wheat shall succeed to clover; oats to fallow;
Roots after wheat be grown";
Such arbitrary dates and rules are vain;
Not thus the year's arithmetic is planned,
But to outwit the cunning of the land
That will not yield, and will not yield again
Her due of food and wealth
Unless the moment's twisted to its use,
Wrung to the utmost by a vigilant hand,
Admitting no unseasonable excuse.

Nevertheless with spring come certain tasks,   *Sowing*
The sowing of crops, as last year's store sinks low. *of crops*
Watch for the day when well-conditioned tilth,
—Run by the winter frost, made sweet by rain,—
Crumbles beneath the foot, and warmly basks
In open fields between the budding shaws;

Sowing Such time when first the rainbow spans its arch
of crops And settling plover wheel, and ragged daws
Firk on the plough, in the first fair days of March,
With the faint tinkle of a wether's bell;
Days when the sky is wide and pale,
Washed by shed rain, swept clear of cloud
By a forgotten gale;
Bare twiggy copses, uplands newly ploughed,
Cart-tracks, gate-gaps in hedges, everything
Wearing its winter aspect with a difference
Not visible to eye, (not visible
Save in close seeing, in the burgeoning
Of a myriad black and thorny joints,)
Still spare and wintry to the outward eye,
But with what change to the sense,
What readiness, what waiting; the suspense
Of earth laid open, naked to the spring.
Such days as these the wary man appoints
For sowing where his earlier foresight tilled,
And harrows cleared the ground of couch and stones.
Yet will his patience still endure delay
If weather's contrary; let boisterous March go by,
And even April temper into May
Before he entrusts the furrow straitly drilled
With precious grain. He knows the clay,
Malevolent, unkind, a spiteful slave;
Has he not felt its rancour in his bones?
Gashed it with share and mattock? torn its flesh?

Has he not stood beside some new-dug grave *Sowing*
In that same churchyard where himself shall lie *of crops*
And seen the yellow pit? the clods turned fresh?
And shall he entrust his summer's hope, his pence,
His cattle's fodder, and his children's bread,
Rashly to that inhospitable bed?

No, rather shall he leave his land unsown
A month or more, if acres will not dry.
Occasion's always timely, not so haste;
And month from month takes many an usurer's loan.
So, with his pocket full of tricks,
His dodges girded on, his cunning braced,
He waits his time, to master and defeat,
For he, like other men, must live by politics.
Thus, if the autumn rains have drowned his wheat,
He shall put oats in April in its stead;
Or if a field be obstinate in weeds,
Set clearing crops from February to June:
Roots that will shelter partridges, and swedes,
And mangolds orange as the harvest-moon.
So shall he fill his barns and build his ricks,
Sowing in spring his barley, oats, and seeds,
(But in the autumn, wheat, and the neglected rye,) *Rotation*
And ever shall he bear in mind the art *of crops*
Known to the Roman, of a changing crop,
To keep his land in kindly heart,
Following wheat on clover, roots on grain,

Rotation Fallow on cereal, as he judges best
of crops To restore his weary land and give it rest,
And spare the toiling of his horse and cart
With dung to spread. So shall he make his gain
And please his fields, and profits shall not drop
Nor men be idle.

Hops   Yet another care,
The pruning and the training of the hop,
Busies the farmer while the year is young.
When bines are cut and cleaned, and poles are bare,
And the loam is richly black with farmyard dung,
Then comes the pruning-knife, and severs clean
Unwanted shoots; the young, too prodigal green
Falls cut, and sadly wilts
There on the ground; but then with balls of twine
Come men on high, strapped stilts,
Woodenly walking, taller than the poles,
Pocking the ground with small round holes,
To tie the string to train the chosen bine,
With a little crawling gang of boys
Busily tying in amongst the hills.
But all's not over then; the rapid plant
Wreathing its spiral upright or aslant,
This delicate tendrilled thing, this English vine
Has baleful foes that prey:
Aphis, that bitter poison kills,
And mould, that sulphur-dust destroys.
So against knave and thief

34

Work with unsparing hand your sulphur spray,   *Hops*
In early morning when the dew
Lies on the sickened leaf,
Till the clean air with yellow powder fills,
And the bare garden floats in dusty gold;
Not once, but be you watchful to renew
Strife against insect, battle against mould.

Look, too, to your orchards in the early spring.   *Or-*
The blossom-weevil bores into the sheath,   *chards*
Grubs tunnel in the pith of promising shoots,
The root-louse spends his winter tucked beneath
Rough bark of trunks or chinks of tangled roots;
Canker, rot, scab, and mildew blight the tree;
There seems an enemy in everything.
Even the bulfinch with his pretty song,
And blue puffed tits make havoc in the pears
Pecking with tiny beak and strong;
Mild February airs
Are full of rogues on mischievous wing,
And orchard trees are wickedly tenanted
By crawling pirates newly roused from sloth,
The apple-sucker and wood-leopard moth.
Who'd win his fight must wage a constant war,
Have sense in his fingers, eyes behind his head;
Therefore let foresight race ahead of time,
Spray close and well

Or-
chards
With soap and sulphur, quassia, lead, and lime,
When buds begin to swell,
All to defeat some small conspirator.

Sometimes in apple country you may see
A ghostly orchard standing all in white,
Aisles of white trees, white branches, in the green,
On some still day when the year hangs between
Winter and spring, and heaven is full of light.
And rising from the ground pale clouds of smoke
Float through the trees and hang upon the air,
Trailing their wisps of blue like a swelled cloak
From the round cheeks of breezes. But though fair
To him who leans upon the gate to stare
And muse "How delicate in spring they be,
That mobled blossom and that wimpled tree,"
There is a purpose in the cloudy aisles
That took no thought of beauty for its care.
For here's the beauty of all country miles,
Their rolling pattern and their space:
That there's a reason for each changing square,
Here sleeping fallow, there a meadow mown,
All to their use ranged different each year,
The shaven grass, the gold, the brindled roan,
Not in some search for empty grace,
But fine through service and intent sincere.

Nor shall you for your fields neglect your stock;   *Young*
Spring is the season when the young things thrive,   *Stock*
Having the kindly months before them. Lambs,
Already sturdy, straggle from the flock;
Frisk tails; tug grass-tufts; stare at children; prance;
Then panic-stricken scuttle for their dams.
Calves learn to drink from buckets; foals
Trot laxly in the meadow, with soft glance
Inquisitive; barn, sty and shed
Teem with young innocence newly come alive.
Round collie puppies, on the sunny step,
Buffet each other with their duffer paws
And pounce at flies, and nose the plaited skep,
And with tucked tail slink yelping from the hive.
Likewise the little secret beasts
That open eyes on a world of death and dread,
Thirst, hunger, and mishap,
The covert denizens of holts and shaws,
The little creatures of the ditch and hedge,
Mice nested in a tussock, shrews, and voles,
Inhabitants of the wood,
The red-legged dabchick, paddling in the sedge,
Followed by chubby brood;
The vixen, prick-eared for the first alarm
Beside her tumbling cubs at foot of tree,—
All in the spring begin their precarious round,
Not cherished as the striplings on the farm,
Sheltered, and cosseted, and kept from harm,

Wild
Creatures
But fang and claw against them, snare and trap,
For life is perilous to the small wild things,
Danger's their lot, and fears abound;
Great cats destroy unheedful wings,
And nowhere's safety on the hunted ground;
And who's to blame them, though they be
Sly, as a man would think him shame?
Man in security walks straight and free,
And shall not measure blame,
For they, that each on other preys,
Weasel on rabbit, owl on shrew,
Their cowardly and murderous ways
In poor defence of life pursue,
Not for a wanton killing, not for lust,
As stags will fight among the trampled brake
With antlers running red; with gore and thrust,
With hoofs that stamp, and royal heads that shake
Blood from their eyes,—in vain,
Since still their splendid anger keeps them blind,
And lowers their entangled brows again,
For brief possession of a faithless hind:—
Not thus, but furtive through the rustling leaves
Life preys on little life; the frightened throat
Squeals once beneath the yellow bite of stoat,
Destroyers all, necessity of kind;
Talon rips fur, and fang meets sharper fang,
And even sleeping limbs must be alert.
But fortunate, if death with sudden pang

Leaps, and is ended; if no lingering hurt,   *Wild*
Dragging a broken wing or mangled paw,   *Creatures*
Brings the slow anguish that no night reprieves,
In the dark refuge of a lonely shaw.

So do they venture on their chance of life   *Young*
When months seem friendliest; so shall men   *Stock*
Repair their herds in spring by natural law
In byre and farrowing pen.
Thus shall you do, with calves that you would rear,
—Heifer, not driven to the slaughterer's knife,
And bull-calf, early cut from bull to steer,—
Two to one udder run, till they may feed
Alone; then turn the foster-siblings out;
Or wean from birth, and teach to drink from pail,
With fair allowance of their mother's milk,
(But watch, for as the calf grows hale,
He's rough, and knocks the empty pail about.)
By either method shall you safely breed
Moist muzzles, thrifty coats of silk,
Well-uddered heifers, bullocks strong and stout.

The wise man, too, will keep his stock of bees   *Bee-*
In a sheltered corner of his garden patch,   *Master*
Where they may winter warmly, breed and hatch
New swarms to fill his combs and fertilize his trees.

I have known honey from the Syrian hills
Stored in cool jars; the wild accacia there

Bee-
Master On the rough terrace where the locust shrills,
Tosses her spindrift to the ringing air;
Narcissus bares his nectarous perianth
In white and golden tabard to the sun,
And while the workers rob the amaranth
Or scarlet windflower low among the stone
Intent upon their crops,
The Syrian queens mate in the high hot day,
Rapt visionaries of creative fray,
Soaring from fecund ecstasy alone,
While through the blazing ether, drops
Like a small thunderbolt the vindicated drone.

I have known bees within the ruined arch
Of Akbar's crimson city hang their comb;
Swarm in forsaken courts in a sultry March,
Where the mild ring-doves croon, and small apes play,
And the thin mangy jackal makes his home;
And where, the red walls kindling in the flares,
Once the great Moghul lolling on his throne,
Between his languid fingers crumbling spice,
Ordered his women to the chequered squares,
And moved them at the hazard of the dice.

But this is the bee-master's reckoning
In England. Walk among the hives and hear.

Forget not bees in winter, though they sleep,
For winter's big with summer in her womb,

And when you plant your rose-trees, plant them deep, *Bee-*
Having regard to bushes all aflame, *Master*
And see the dusky promise of their bloom
In small red shoots, and let each redolent name—
Tuscany, Crested Cabbage, Cottage Maid—
Load with full June November's dank repose;
See the kind cattle drowsing in the shade,
And hear the bee about his amorous trade,
Brown in the gipsy crimson of the rose.

In February, if the days be clear,
The waking bee, still drowsy on the wing,
Will guess the opening of another year
And blunder out to seek another spring.
Crashing through winter sunlight's pallid gold,
His clumsiness sets catkins on the willow
Ashake like lambs' tails in the early fold,
Dusting with pollen all his brown and yellow,
But when the rimy afternoon turns cold
And undern squalls buffet the chilly fellow,
He'll seek the hive's warm waxen welcoming
And set about the chambers' classic mould.

And then pell-mell his harvest follows swift,
Blossom and borage, lime and balm and clover,
On Downs the thyme, on cliffs the scantling thrift,
Everywhere bees go racing with the hours,
For every bee becomes a drunken lover,

41

Bee-
Master   Standing upon his head to sup the flowers.
All over England, from Northumbrian coasts,
To the wild sea-pink blown on Devon rocks,
Over the merry southern gardens, over
The grey-green bean-fields, round the Kentish oasts,
Through the frilled spires of cottage hollyhocks,
Go the big brown fat bees, and wander in
Where dusty spears of sunlight cleave the barn,
And seek the sun again, and storm the whin,
And in the warm meridian solitude
Hum in the heather round the moorland tarn.

Look, too, when summer hatches out the brood,
In tardy May or early June,
And the young queens are strong in the cocoon,
Watch, if the days be warm,
The flitting of the swarm.
Follow, for if beyond your sight they stray,
Your bees are lost, and you must take your way
Homeward disconsolate; but be at hand
And you may take your bees on strangers' land.
Have your skep ready, drowse them with your smoke;
Whether they cluster on the handy bough
Or in the difficult hedge, be nimble now,
For bees are captious folk
And quick to turn against the lubber's touch,
But if you shake them to their wicker hutch
Firmly, and turn towards the hive your skep,

Into the hive the clustered thousands stream,
Mounting the little slatted sloping step,
A ready colony, queen, workers, drones,
Patient to build again the waxen thrones
For younger queens, and all the chambered cells
For lesser brood, and all the immemorial scheme.

Bee-
Master

And still they labour, though the hand of man
Inscrutable and ravaging descend,
Pillaging in their citadels,
Defeating wantonly their provident plan,
Making a havoc of their patient hoard;
Still silly bees, not knowing to what end,
Not knowing to what ultimate reward
Or what new ruin of the garnered hive
The senseless god in man will send,
Still in blind stupid industry will strive,
Constructing for destruction pitiably,
That still their unintelligible lord
May reap his wealth from their calamity.

White virgin honey comes from earliest flowers,
White virgin honey in the market prized;
From the white clover creeping in the field,
From orchard-blossom that the worker scours,
—The richest honey-flow of all the Weald,—
But cottage-gardens shall not be despised
Here where no heather is, and scanty lime;
Therefore, at evening, when the field-work's done,

43

Bee-
Master
And daylight lingers with the latening sun,
Let gardeners too remember sowing-time.

Gar-
dener
When skies are gentle, breezes bland,
When loam that's warm within the hand
Falls friable between the tines,
Sow hollyhocks and columbines,
The tufted pansy, and the tall
Snapdragon in the broken wall,
Not for this summer, but for next,
Since foresight is the gardener's text,
And though his eyes may never know
How lavishly his flowers blow,
Others will stand and musing say
"These were the flowers he sowed that May."

But for this summer's quick delight
Sow marigold, and sow the bright
Frail poppy that with noonday dies
But wakens to a fresh surprise;
Along the pathway stones be set
Sweet Alysson and mignonette,
That when the full midsummer's come
On scented clumps the bees may hum,
Golden Italians, and the wild
Black humble-bee alike beguiled:
And lovers who have never kissed
May sow the cloudy Love-in-Mist.

44

Nor be the little space forgot   *Gar-*
For herbs to spice the kitchen pot: *dener*
Mint, pennyroyal, bergamot,
Tarragon and melilot,
Dill for witchcraft, prisoners' rue,
Coriander, costmary,
Tansy, thyme, Sweet Cicely,
Saffron, balm, and rosemary
That since the Virgin threw her cloak
Across it,—so say cottage folk—
Has changed its flowers from white to blue.
But have a care that seeds be strewn
One night beneath a waxing moon,
And pick when the moon is on the wane,
Else shall your toil be all in vain.

She walks among the loveliness she made,   *The*
Between the apple-blossom and the water—   *Island*
She walks among the patterned pied brocade,
Each flower her son, and every tree her daughter.
This is an island all with flowers inlaid,
A square of grassy pavement tessellated;
Flowers in their order blowing as she bade,
And in their company by her created.
The waving grasses freckle sun with shade,
The wind-blown waters round the kingcups ripple,
Colour on colour chequered and arrayed,
Shadow on light in variable stipple.

45

The
Island

Her regiments at her command parade,
Foot-soldier primrose in his rank comes trooping,
Then wind-flowers in a scarlet loose brigade,
Fritillary with dusky orchis grouping.
They are the Cossacks, dim in ambuscade,
Scarfed in their purple like a foreign stranger,
Piratical, and apt for stealthy raid,
Wherever's mystery or doubtful danger.
Iris salutes her with his broad green blade,
And marches by with proud imperial pennant,
And tulips in a flying cavalcade
Follow valerian for their lieutenant.
The Lords-and-Ladies dressed for masquerade
In green silk domino discreetly hooded,
Hurry towards the nut-trees' colonnade,
Philandering where privacy's well wooded;
They're the civilians of this bold crusade,
The courtiers of this camp by blossom tented,
With woodbine clambering the balustrade,
And all by briar roses battlemented.
There, in the sunlit grasses green as jade,
She walks; she sees her squadrons at attention,
And, laughing at her flowery escapade,
Stretches her hands towards her dear invention.

The wild
flowers

This much of gardens; but I tell
Also of native flowers in wood and dell;

46

Not such as, sudden on a stony height,   *The*
Break from the warmth of snow and live in light   *wild*
Of mountain sun on Alp or Dolomite,   *flowers*
Bright squabs on limestone screes;
Not of the Rhoetian poppy, fluttering brave
Frail yellow flags beside a rocky track
Alone with eagles; not of these,
Not of the thymes that greenly pave
A fallen cliff, rock-rose in cruel crack;
Not of the scarlet tulip, slim and bright,
Snapped by the gallop of the gay gazelle;
But of such flowers as dwell
In marsh and meadow, wayside, wood and waste,
Of campion and the little pimpernel;
Of kexen parsley and the varied vetch;
Of the living mesh, cats-cradle in a ditch;
Of gorse and broom and whins;
Of hops and buckwheat and the wild woodbine
That with their stems must twine
Like the way of the sun to left from right;
Of berried bindweeds, twisting widdershins;
Of all the tangle of the hedgerow, laced
With thorny dog-rose and the deadly dwale;
Throughout the seasons do I count their tale,
But orderly, that those who walk abroad
In lane and wood   *The*
May find them in their season as they grow;   *wood-*
Anemones like some last drift of snow   *flowers*

47

The   Between the hazels, hanging down their bell
wood- When rain's about; small woodruff low;
flowers Bugles, that leave the shelter of the glade
       And march across the open; violets that blow
       Purple and dim at tree's-foot; and the tall
       Orchis that country children call
       By many names, some pretty and some rude.
       These are the flowers that shelter in the wood,
       Sulky in colour, as secret in the shade;
The   But wayside tramps, saucy and unafraid,
wayside Jack-by-the-hedge, Pickpocket, Ragged Robin,
flowers Small yellows and small scarlets, nowise strange,
       Nowise like aliens strayed,
       But English and robust,
       Fight tangled for their life through grit and dust,
       Pushing their way with spring, when heifers range
       Uneasy up the lane, and as they go
       Tug at a passing mouthful, biting harsh.
       And others in the meadow and the marsh
       Make rings round Easter; kingcup, marigold,
       And the pale orchis dappled like a dobbin;
       Buttercups thousand-fold
       Wearing their cloth-of-gold among the hay
       With clover and the little eye-of-day.

Fritil- But once I went through the lanes, over the sharp
laries Tilt of the little bridges; past the forge,
       And heard the clang of anvil and of iron,

And saw the founting sparks in the dusky forge,
And men outside with horses, gossiping.
So I came through that April England, moist
And green in its lush fields between the willows,
Foaming with cherry in the woods, and pale
With clouds of lady's-smock along the hedge,
Until I came to a gate and left the road
For the gentle fields that enticed me, by the farms,
Wandering through the embroidered fields, each one
So like its fellow; wandered through the gaps,
Past the mild cattle knee-deep in the brook,
And wandered drowsing as the meadows drowsed
Under the pale wide heaven and slow clouds.
And then I came to a field where the springing grass
Was dulled by the hanging cups of fritillaries,
Sullen and foreign-looking, the snaky flower,
Scarfed in dull purple, like Egyptian girls
Camping among the furze, staining the waste
With foreign colour, sulky-dark and quaint,
Dangerous too, as a girl might sidle up,
An Egyptian girl, with an ancient snaring spell,
Throwing a net, soft round the limbs and heart,
Captivity soft and abhorrent, a close-meshed net,
—See the square web on the murrey flesh of the
    flower—
Holding her captive close with her bare brown arms.
Close to her little breast beneath the silk,
A gipsy Judith, witch of a ragged tent,

*Fritil-
laries*

49

Fritil- And I shrank from the English field of fritillaries
laries Before it should be too late, before I forgot
      The cherry white in the woods, and the curdled clouds,
      And the lapwings crying free above the plough.

Spring The spring was late that year, I well remember,
      The year when first I came on the field of fritillaries;
      So late, the cottars meeting in the lanes
      Would stop to marvel mildly, with that old
      Unplumbed capacity for wonderment
      At Nature's whim. The calendar told spring,
      But spring was heedless: April into May
      Passed, and the trees still wore their livery
      Of lean black winter's servants; very strange
      Most lovely Easter played three days at summer,
      A heavy summer over winter's fields,
      Three days, and then was vanished, like a queen
      Dropping the lifted flap of her pavilion.

      Nightly I leant me at the window-sill,
      Telling the chaplet of the slipping days,
      But still the lamp streamed wet on polished stones,
      And still the nights were empty silences
      Robbed of the nightingale; they only held
      The slanting strings of rain: Orion marched
      Invisible down the hours from dusk to dawn,
      Till morning pallor lost him, but the clouds

Hid all his gradual latening; that year   *Spring*
He shot his midnight javelins unseen
And dipped the horizon into other skies,
Lost to the North, till autumn should renew
His captaincy, with Rigel, Betelgeuse,
Aldebaran, and brightest Sirius.

Have we so many springs allotted us,
And who would rob a pauper of his pence?

Then broke the spring. The hedges in a day
Burgeoned to green; the drawing of the trees,
Incomparably pencilled line by line,
Thickened to heaviness, and men forgot
The intellectual austerity
Of winter, in the rich warm-blooded rush
Of growth, and mating beasts, and rising sap.
How swift and sudden strode that tardy spring,
Between a sunrise and a sunset come!
The shadow of a swallow crossed the wall;
Nightingales sang by day. The pushing blade
Parted the soil. The morning roofs and oasts
There, down the lane, beside the brook and willows,
Cast their long shadows. Pasture, ankle-wet,
Steamed to the sun. The tulips dyed their green
To red in cottage gardens. Bees astir,
Fussing from flower to flower, made war on time.
Body and blood were princes; the cold mind

Spring Sank with Orion from the midnight sky;
The stars of spring rose visible: The Virgin;
Al Fard the solitary; Regulus
The kingly star, the handle of the Sickle;
And Venus, lonely splendour in the west,
Roamed over the rapt meadows; shone in gold
Beneath the cottage eaves where nesting birds
Obeyed love's law; shone through the cottage panes
Where youth lay sleeping on the breast of youth,
Where love was life, and not a brief desire;
Shone on the heifer blaring for the bull
Over the hedgerow deep in dewy grass:
And glinted through the dark and open door
Where the proud stallion neighing to his mares
Stamped on the cobbles of the stable floor.
For all were equal in the sight of spring,
Man and his cattle; corn; and greening trees,
Ignorant of the soul's perplexity,
Ignorant of the wherefore and the end,
Bewildered by no transient ecstasy,
But following the old and natural law,
Nor marred nor blazing with a royal excess;
The law of life and life's continuance.

That was a spring of storms. They prowled the night;
Low level lightning flickered in the east
Continuous. The white pear-blossom gleamed
Motionless in the flashes; birds were still;

52

Darkness and silence knotted to suspense,   *Spring*
Riven by the premonitory glint
Of skulking storm, a giant that whirled a sword
Over the low horizon, and with tread
Earth-shaking ever threatened his approach,
But to delay his terror kept afar,
And held earth stayed in waiting like a beast
Bowed to receive a blow. But when he strode
Down from his throne of hills upon the plain,
And broke his anger to a thousand shards
Over the prostrate fields, then leapt the earth
Proud to accept his challenge; drank his rain;
Under his sudden wind tossed wild her trees;
Opened her secret bosom to his shafts;
The great drops spattered; then above the house
Crashed thunder, and the little wainscot shook
And the green garden in the lightning lay.

Who has not seen the spring, is blind, is dead.
Better for him that he should coffined lie
And in that coin his toll to Nature pay
Than live a debtor. All things shall pass by
That fret his mind: the shift of policy,
Princes' ambition, wiser governance,
Civilisation's tides. There's dissonance
By our great necessary Babel bred,
Perplexes eager spirits unprepared,
Puts out their seeing eyes, leaves their blind touch

Spring   To grope past prejudice and ignorance
Towards solution, as they throw away
Each broken, each successive crutch.
Such truths as we have snared
Into the spread conspiracy of our nets,
Come to us fragmentary from a whole,
As meteorites from space. Now science sets
Two splintered ends together, makes one shred
Corroborate another; now live flesh
Persuades us by its drunken fallacy;
Now the instinctive soul
Takes its short-cut to grace; now blown by gust
Of hazard, truth's entangled in strange mesh,
Else how should poetry,
The runes of divination, superstition
Fastening sharp claw on common circumstance,
Even artifice as neat astrology
Twisting the very stars to fit man's ends,
Mingle some ore with dross of sorcery
Unless the fragment of the whole be part?
There's some relation we may not adjust,
Some concord of creation that the mind
Only in perilous balance apprehends,
Loth, fugitive, obscure.
All else dies in its season; all perplexities,
Even human grief with the human body dies,
Such griefs that press so wildly on the heart
As to crush in its shell. But still endure

Nature's renewal and man's fortitude,   *Spring*
A common thing, a permanent common thing,
So coarse, so stated, usual, and so rude,
So quiet in performance, and so slow
That hurrying wit outruns it. Yet with spring
Life leaps; her fountains flow;
And nimble foolish wit must humbled go.

There were so many days that I was given.
But whether of this spring or that? they merge
As travelling clouds across my permanent heaven.

My life was rich; I took a swarm of bees
And found a crumpled snake-skin on the road,
All in one day, and was increased by these.

I have not understood humanity.
But those plain things, that gospel of each year,
Made me the scholar of simplicity.

This once I saw, but not again,
Above the water pocked by rain:
Three mottled eggs in a moorhen's nest,
In a clump of kingcups by the edge
Of the water, in amongst the sedge;
The rain was but an April shower;
The kingcup but a minted flower,
Cup of a king in gold.

Spring   *Was there not once a king who sought him*
        The perfect chalice, and bethought him
        The breast of Helen for his mould?
        A wild bird's nest and Helen's breast,
        What lovely things that spring did hold!

*   *   *   *   *   *   *

Noc-   Now die the sounds. No whisper stirs the trees.
turne   Her pattern merged into the general web
       The shriven day accepts her obsequies
         With humble ebb.

Now are the noiseless stars made visible
   That hidden by the day pursued their track,
And this one planet that we know too well
   Mantles in black.

Then, from the thicket, sang the nightingale,
   So wildly sweet, so sudden, and so true,
It seemed a herald from beyond the veil
   Had broken through.

The common earth's confusion all unseen,
   But worlds revealed in broad magnificence,—
That unembodied music thrid between
   Sprang hence, or thence?

Nothing remained of the familiar round,
  Only the soul ecstatic and released
Founted towards the spheres in jets of sound,
  And died, and ceased,

But plangent from the thickets of the thorn
  Broke other voices, taking up the choir,
While Cancer interlaced with Capricorn
  In silent fire,

And all the harmonies were joined and whole,
  Silence was music, music silence made,
Till each was both or either, and the soul
  Was not afraid.

Nocturne

SUMMER

SUMMER

Now be you thankful, who in England dwell,
That to the starving trees and thirsty grass
Even at summer's height come cloudy fleets
Moist from the wastes of the Atlantic swell,
To spill their rain, and pass,
While fields renew their sweets.
Not as the Arab watches in despair
The scrannel promise of his harvest parch
Even before the sun climbs high in March
And only dust-motes dim the scorching air,
He who must yoke to wooden water-wheel
The bullock or the camel, turning slow
But constant in the round and trodden groove,
Slumberous as hypnotics move,
To the lamentation of the whining cogs,
While in the runnels rapid waters flow,
Lapped by the timid tongue of pariah dogs,
And in the trenches spread, to quench and heal.
Or as the Persian from his hills of snow
Gathers the freshet to the jealous pool,
And floods his garden with a hundred streams
Under the plane-trees when the evening's cool,

But still for all his pains
Sees roses languish with returning noon,
And in the heat of June
The leaves already flutter from the planes.

Such arid months as only exiles know,
With longing for the smell of English rains,
Some drops to lay the dust, some shower to stir
The earthy redolence of soaking loam,
Some saddening of the sky before the shower,
Some dew to hold a footprint for an hour;
When through the stones the lizard and the snake
Rustle their brittle length, and crickets chirr
Day after day, and broom-pods crackling break,
Scavenger kites hang waiting for the dead
Over the old and solitary ram,
And the mule picks his way up the dried river-bed,—
This know, and know then how the heart can ache
With pining for the woods and clouds of home.

If I could take my England, and could wring
One living moment from her simple year,
One moment only, whether of place or time,
—One winter coppice feathery with rime,
One shred of dawn in spring,—
Then should my voice find echo in English ear;
Then might I say, "That which I love, I am."

62

Full summer comes; June brings the longest day.
All country dwellers know the small despair
Of the year's summit; but the yeoman now
Has little time for vain regrets to spare.
There's work enough for him and all his folks;
He watches for the flowering of his hay;
Knows that cleared land is ready for the plough;
Washes his empty sheds with cleansing lime
While herds at pasture fatten to their prime,
With fisking tails in shade beneath the oaks.

Before great harvest takes him to the field, *Sheep*
Imperious and urgent for his time, *Shearing*
If he be wise he'll finish with his flock
Shearing as early as the warmth of May
Down in the genial meadows of the Weald.
There, in a barn, with crazy doors swung wide
Making a square of sun on dusty floor,
The shearer sits, in shepherd's borrowed smock,
And from the pen of huddled backs outside,
Each beast in turn is driven through the door;
Struggles, and kicks, but with a hands-twist thrown
Lies foolish, as the fingers slick and deft
Open the fleece and cut the belly up,
(Changing left hand for right, and right for left,)
Against the fall of wool, in one sole piece,
All test of skill, all source of surly pride;
Then on the heap is pitched the greasy fleece,

Sheep And the clipped sheep,—hogg, wether, lusty tup,—
Shearing Staggers astonished from such curt release,
And bleating seeks the refuge of the heft;
Naked, and bleating, and at first forlorn
With narrow smear of blood on neck or side,
From sharp experience goes the shearling shorn.

Shep- Yet is the shepherd roughly kind;
herd Anoints a wound, shakes disapproving head,
But tolerant, to slight mishap resigned;
Scours the short wool for maggot, tick, or ked.
Shepherd's an old and a familiar trade;
Abel, that firstling of the sunburnt plains,
Through the scorched months between the annual rains
Sang to his firstlings in the fig-tree's shade;
As Jacob, seven years to win a maid,
—She being beautiful, and Leah but tender-eyed,—
Drove out his flock into the stony place,
Ringstraked, speckled, pied;
Peeled the green poplar switch, and dreamed of Rachel's
        face;
As David, young and ruddy, kept the sheep,
Shepherd and harp-player in the wilderness;
Shaping for kingship, growing to a throne,
Come from the wilds to soothe dark Saul to sleep.
For no man knows as he who lives alone
The vigour of a purpose deeply laid,
The strength, the fate, the seal upon his brow,

The urgency of an unpublished vow,
A vow unregistered, a vow unmade,
Unknown to its maker, rather; only known
To the God and origin of such fumbling ends,
So inly lived, so congruously held,
True in each gesture as by force compelled,
(For no man sees the pattern of his maze,
Least of all he who plans his careful ways
Lacking the strong inevitable thing,)
As Israel, Abel, David knew,
Yet unaware to consummation grew,
The patriarch, the martyr, and the king.

No man is closer to the beasts he tends,
Nor, idle, savours such contented days;
No man more blessèd-free,
Free from our need of comfort and of friends,
Love, props, illusion, counterfeit, escape;
Living a life that to its real shape
Evolves, increases, swells its girth, ascends,
As an unconscious and a splendid tree,
A fact of Nature, not a random plan.

I remember, I met two shepherds carrying
An old man, dead, high on the summer Downs.
He was a shepherd too; I had known the man.
Foxes he knew, he knew the ways of the hawk,

*Shep-
herd*

Shep-
herd
The ways of weather, but not the ways of towns.
Dead now, his white flock going before
With shaken bells across the scars of chalk,
His dog at heel of the man who propped his head.
I stopped to gaze, since I should gaze no more;
To take my last look, since here was no returning,
But could not learn from him, for there's no learning
Either from alien or familiar dead.

Sheep
Washing
After the general shearing still remain
The tenderer milch-yoes to be clipped.
A separate job, some later week,
When temperate days will hold,
—For eild sheep, wethers, hoggs, and barren yoes
Risk with less danger the returning cold.
Then may the lambs be dipped,
The lambs that frantic for their mothers seek,
And gaunt, ungainly, queer, regain the fold.
And general dipping next in order goes,
Snatched between hay and harvest, as may be,
And as the ripening and the weather fit.
This is a feast that makes the whole farm shout
With laughter as on holiday, to see
The bothered and unwilling beasts submit
And swim the tank, and scramble dripping out
With never a maggot left, or louse, or flea.
Sheep do the work, while men stand grinning by,

Knowing that work in earnest waits them after
This interlude, this funning, and this laughter,
Work in the fields, with aching thews, and sweat,
And blessed coolth only when sun has set.

Sheep
Washing

The summer's horn indeed is full with crops;
And earlier toil its due reward has earned.
Now shall you reap and gather, store and stack
Your hay, your corn, your barley and your hops
In close succession, being less concerned
With calendar and farmer's almanac
Than with good timely weather, setting fair
Over the parcelled fields from copse to copse;
Good summer sun, that dries the waggon track,
Ripens the grasses, tans the swollen awn,
And puts contented faces everywhere.

Haysel
and
Harvest

First you shall cut your hay, when grasses stand
In flower, but running not to seed,
But even here rehearse the farmer's creed:
'Tis farmer, not the date, that calls the tune;
Better dry August hay than wet in June.
Have your folks working in the fields by dawn,
Your team of horses doubly spanned;
Leave the cut swath all day; and air by rake
Next morning, and, if weather still be set,
Gather to cocks for carting, but should wet

Haysel

Haysel   Flatten the cocks, then you shall tedd and shake
Again when sun returns. Now you shall build
Your rick in yard or field, as suits you best,
Choosing your stacker for a good man skilled,
Building on brushwood, sides both true and straight,
That when hay settles lines may still be plumb;
And let each forkful to its place be pressed
And truly bound, by stacker's treading weight;
Widen your eaving-course; let roof be steep,
Bents sloping outwards, so to keep
Rain from the heart until the thatcher come.
Then you may leave your rick with easy mind;
Fodder for sweet-breathed cattle shall be sweet;
And whether nights be harsh or days be kind
Your hay shall neither moulder, rot, nor heat;
You shall not wake to hear your cowman shout,
As calving heifer calls him from his rest;
You shall not stare to see in fear and doubt
A blood-red feather flaming on the west,
And rousing all your people as you run,
Hasten too late towards your labour's pyre,
And see your reckoned trusses, hardly-won,
Blaze to the wanton merriment of fire.

Next shall you reap your corn. Your oats shall fall
Before full ripeness set them on to shed,
But leave your barley till it droop the head
With ripened beard. The tall

68

Wheat for an early cut; at midday, walk   *Harvest*
When sun is hot and high, and if you hear
Straw crackle in the standing crop,
And see the slender forest of the stalk
Still green towards the ground, but gold at top,
Then you may know that cutting-time is near.
Peas are pernickety; cut when you may.
Beans, the sweet-scented beans of spring, shall stand
Till pods are turning black, or till you clear
Against the needs of autumn for your land.
Now as to cutting: you shall choose your day
When weather signs are fairest, as for hay;
Scythe first the heading round the field by hand,
Then send your reaper up the flat gold wall
With whirling sails and clash of toppling sheaves;
See that the cutter keen and sharply cleaves,
And that the horses, driven with a level gait,
Work the full width, and keep the measure straight.

And in the evening when the final square
Of standing corn fast dwindles to its end,
When the tired horses take a sharper bend,
A shorter strip each time, as day grows late,
Let boys stand round, with ready stick and stone,
Watching for dash of rabbit or of hare
Within the last small narrowing refuge penned;
Poor frightened Wat, that all the day alone
(Since first the reaper with its whirring noise

Harvest Made terror of the field,)
Crouched to the ground, by friendly straw concealed,
Inward and inward creeping, as the voice
Of men came nearer, and the sheaves were thrown
Out on the widening stubble, there to lie
Until the stooker with his fork came by,
And horses' shaggy fetlock trampled past
At their monotonous pacing, till at last
Through thinning stalks, pressed flat against the earth,
The fugitive saw, with starting eye,
Their shining shoes strike fire on errant flints,
And the sharp knives slip by with level glints.
Then goes the lean brown body for its life,
Streaked for the distant shelter of the wood,
Across the new, strange stubble hurled,
That was not there at dawn,—a different world
Since men and horses came with cutting knife,
And razed the corn that tall and rustling stood.
But odds too heavy end the frantic race;
There's nothing but a twitching body cast
Down by a jacket, as 'twere nothing worth
But shillings to the farmer's frugal wife.

An English cornfield in full harvesting
Is English as the Bible, though no more
(These clanking times) the gleaners following
The reapers by their rhythm rapt
Plunder the gavels for their little store;

70

Or the sickle cut the poppies and the corn,   *Harvest*
Save when the crop is tangled by a gale,
Beaten by rain, twisted like murdered hair:
Then comes the sickle to its old avail
Crook'd as the young moon in her narrowest horn,
And steals in the poor broken tangle, where
Straightforward knives are parried, and the apt
Inventiveness of man shall not prevail.
Then to the simplest shapes of his first craft,
—Livelihood wrested from the earth that bore,
Cradled, and coffined him,—man shall repair;
Shapes copied from the sky, with cutting edge;
Natural shapes, to meet the natural hitch
Of hindering weather, the permanent enemy;
Then, with the noonscape, underneath the hedge,
His fingers blistered by the rubbing haft,
His shoulders propped by hedge, his feet in ditch,
The random reaper drains his pint of ale.

Look to your stooking, for full many a field
Of hearty grain and straw runs half to waste
Through heedless stooking, and the proper yield
Leaves half its measure to the rook and daw.
But if you'd have full grain and ripened straw,
After a week of drying fit to cart,
Stooker, take up a sheaf in either hand,
Between the ears and band,
And swing them clear, and bring the butts apart

71

Harvest   Sharply to ground, ears sloping to a peak,
(Ten sheaves for Kent,) clashing together, braced,
So that the little ridge be thatched and sleek,
Firm to the wind, secure to rain and hail,
That winnower and that flail,
Those thieves of harvest, pilfering what they can
In last-hour larceny from rival man.
For nature gives, and nature takes again;
Therefore be eager of her liberal hours;
To drought succeeds the flood, to calm the gale,
And winter's frost lays low the summer's flowers.
Therefore, you harvesters, before the rain
Trample your crop with roguish feet,
Wring what you may, and if too fast and fleet
Even the summer sun describe his arc
Leaving you with your shocks but half-way set,
Be prouder than the punctual rigid clerk,
And stickle not to labour after dark,
For you take nature's orders, he the clock's.
The cooler night shall spare your noonday sweat;
The breeze shall whisper in the rustling shocks;
The moon above the thorn
Rise harvest-tawny on the stubble shorn,
And in the bending lines of girls and men
Some snatch of song be born.
Lovers shall find their magic then,
And jolly farmers wink at privilege;
Only the moon shall look behind the hedge,

72

Confederate of youth; *Harvest*
Only the moon shall hear the whispered pledge,
Great lyric liar, to a lovelier truth
Transcending, setting purport free,
And touching all things with her alchemy.

When moonlight reigns, the meanest brick and stone
Take on a beauty not their own,
And past the flaw of builded wood
Shines the intention whole and good,
And all the little homes of man
Rise to a dimmer, nobler plan
When colour's absence gives escape
To the deeper spirit of the shape.

—Then earth's great architecture swells
Among her mountains and her fells
Under the moon to amplitude
Massive and primitive and rude;

—Then do the clouds like silver flags
Stream out above the tattered crags,
And black and silver all the coast
Marshals its hunched and rocky host,
And headlands striding sombrely
Buttress the land against the sea,
The darkening land, the brightening wave,—
When moonlight slants through Merlin's cave.

Harvest   And August comes, when fields are sere and brown,
When stubble takes the place of ruffling corn;
When the sweet grass is like a prisoner shorn;
The air is full of drifting thistledown,
Grey pointed sprites, that on the breezes ride.
The cloyed trees droop, the ash-keys spinning fall;
The brooks are pebbly, for the trickle's dried;
Birds moult, and in the leafy copses hide,
And summer makes a silence after spring,
As who with age a liberal youth should chide.

Weod-
monath

This is the month of weeds.
Kex, charlock, thistle,
Among the shorn bristle
Of stubble drop seeds.
This is the month of weeds.

Spurry, pimpernel, quitch,
Twine in the stubble,
Making for trouble;
With nettle in ditch,
Spurry, pimpernel, quitch.

Yet the field has a friend,
The nimble clover,
Custodian, lover,
Yare to defend.
The field has a friend.

Humble-bees boldly reach　　　　　　*Weod-*
Red clover's honey,　　　　　　　　*monath*
Paid in sweet money.
Hive-bees in vain beseech:
Honey is out of reach.

Now let the clover spread;
Nature it craveth;
Foemen it braveth,
Strangling them dead.
So let the clover spread.

Now pasture's low; the moidered cattle-men　　*Summer*
Drive their poor stock by unaccustomed paths
To forage on the richer aftermaths,
Old hay-fields, billowy with dip and stetch.
Now by the hedgerows and along the lane
The berried cuckoo-pint and yellow vetch
Herald the autumn, and the squirrels rob
Windfalls of hazel and the Kentish cob,
(Plumping their kernels white as children's teeth,)
With acorns, provender for the winter drey,
That little larder, safely tucked beneath
Leaves, roots, old tree-stumps, for a milder day
Of winter, when the sleeping muscles stretch
And there's a stirring in the sodden wood
As woken squirrel reaches after food.

Summer Man's not the only harvester; urchins, voles
Lay up their store of berries and of grain
Preciously gleaned and carried to their holes
With busy trotting paws and serious snout,
Each to his scheme no less than man devout,
Making of instinct all-sufficient reasons;
Intent on waking with the spring again
To life's new provocation, as if the seasons
Eternally renewed were dedicate
To hedge-hogs, squirrels, badgers, men, mice, moles.

But though such hints of autumn gild the late
Summer, still is the summer fully here,
Great-breasted, brazen, strumpet of the year;
Furiously I do the summer hate,
Resentfully I do the summer love,
The woods all amorous with croodling dove,
Days weakening to the soul, days threatening
Winter-bought strength, thin purity of spring.
With summer's laxness am I all undone.
What can I do in summer? What but sing:

> *Far from shrewd companies,*
> *Far from the flares,*
> *Here where the summer is,*
> *And laden airs,*
> *Here where no noise of men*
> *Down in the wood*

76

Startles the water-hen
And small black brood,
Here where the branches wave
And day is green,
Making the wood a cave
Aquamarine,
Here where the insects hum,
And dragon-fly,
Here we clandestine come,
Marvell and I.

In summer when the woods are deep,
Ghostly society I keep,
And play the spy, down dappled glades,
On lovely or on ardent shades,
Eavesdropper on the gallant game
Where nothing's burnt by so much flame,
And nothing broken but the rhyme
From maying-time to haying-time.
And what's the matter, though I see
A wrongly amorous company?
Though lover after lover flit
Labelled with names that do not fit?
If Lovelace Sacharissa woo,
Or Waller Julia pursue,
If Marvell do Lucasta find
Than his own mistress less unkind,
Or Herrick's persuasions prove

Summer   *A better argument of love*
             Than the conversion of the Jew?

             The cuckoo stutters in his note,
             But still the turbulent petticoat
             Of cherry silk or oyster grey
             Makes lively sport through summer day.
             The rounded arm, the bunchèd curl,
             The peeping shoe, the sullen pearl,—
             Between the trees they glance and pass,
             Or take their ease upon the grass.

             Perilla, fly! Corinna, stay!
             In deserts of Bohemia,
             A wood near Athens, or this wood
             Where these grown oaks as saplings stood
             Three hundred English years gone by,
             "And yet I love her till I die."

So, for the idle, float the lither days,
The seremonth deepens as its age draws on;
Morning and evening veil them in a haze;
But when the last high loaded cart has gone
Leaving its trail of straws along the hedge,
And the last mug is drained to harvest-pledge,
Work still remains to finish what is done.

Thatcher with carpet bound about his knees   *Thatcher*
Tramps farm to farm with slow deliberate stride.
Thatchers are rare, these days, he'd have you know,
Good thatchers, those that go
About their business as it were a pride,
Scorning Dutch barns and mushrooms such as these,
New-fangled, driving out a settled trade.
Once there were thatchers, ah, could hip a roof
Easy as twist a sheaf; were not afraid
Of any rain, since work was weather-proof.
East Anglia bred them, where the reeds grow grey
Mile upon fenny mile, and ducks go home
Over the level wastes of dyke and sluice.
Still maundering on, he sorts his pegs, his comb,
His wooden bat, his twine, in neat array,
Trimming his straw,—full length of wheaten straw,—
Watered and sweated ready to its use,
Sweet in the yelm, for thatch without a flaw.
Grumbling and boasting turn and turn about,
Having told the tally of the needed threaves,
He mounts his ladder, pocket full of splines,
And packs his yelms, and calls his mate a lout
If he disturb one straw from ordered lines.
Proud of his stelch, and prouder of his eaves,
Proud of his skill to thatch an awkward pent,
He is an artist with a long descent,
Brother to workers in peculiar crafts;
To the old wheel-wright, punctual timber-master,

79

Thatcher —Could tell you whether wood were frow or doted
Before the trunk was opened; often quoted
The Bible; could turn out a pair of shafts
With straight and proper grain; adzed every spoke
By hand, and never had one cracked or bent;—
Crafts- Brother to pargetter, with hair and plaster,
men Combing the diaper on porous lime,
Pleased as a child with patterns he'd invent;
Brother to all the slow fastidious folk
Whose care is matched by their disdain of time;
To basket-makers, shaping Kentish bodges;
To osier-weavers, twisting supple wands;
To Jack-of-all-trades with his sundry dodges;
Brick-layer, even, carrying his hod;
To Down-bred shepherds, puddling secret ponds,
So jealous of their mystery, for dew;
Lastly, to dowser, forcing virgin wells,
That changeling of the willows, simple, odd,
Touched by some finger laid on him askew
At birth by nixie or by water-god;
But dowser never knows, or never tells.
Smiling, the willow upright in his hold,
Vacant he lags across the thirsty miles;
Shall water pull him? or shall buried gold,
Panoply of a Dane, beneath a mound?
But dowser never knew, or never told.
Only, he pauses when he feels the switch
Quicken between his fingers, curtsey, twitch;

Pauses, and points, and smiles,
And loses interest; for water's found.

All craftsmen share a knowledge. They have held
Reality down fluttering to a bench;
Cut wood to their own purposes; compelled
The growth of pattern with the patient shuttle;
Drained acres to a trench.
Control is theirs. They have ignored the subtle
Release of spirit from the jail of shape.
They have been concerned with prison, not escape;
Pinioned the fact, and let the rest go free,
And out of need made inadvertent art.
All things designed to play a faithful part
Build up their plain particular poetry.
Tools have their own integrity;
The sneath of scythe curves rightly to the hand,
The hammer knows its balance, knife its edge,
All tools inevitably planned,
Stout friends, with pledge
Of service; with their crotchets too
That masters understand,
And proper character, and separate heart,
But always to their chosen temper true.
—So language, smithied at the common fire,
Grew to its use; as sneath and shank and haft
Of well-grained wood, nice instruments of craft,

Crafts-
men   Curve to the simple mould the hands require,
Born of the needs of man.
The poet like the artisan
Works lonely with his tools; picks up each one,
Blunt mallet knowing, and the quick thin blade,
And plane that travels when the hewing's done;
Rejects, and chooses; scores a fresh faint line;
Sharpens, intent upon his chiselling;
Bends lower to examine his design,
If it be truly made,
And brings perfection to so slight a thing.
But in the shadows of his working-place,
Dust-moted, dim,
Among the chips and lumber of his trade,
Lifts never his bowed head, a breathing-space
To look upon the world beyond the sill,
The world framed small, in distance, for to him
The world and all its weight are in his will.
Yet in the ecstasy of his rapt mood
There's no retreat his spirit cannot fill,
No distant leagues, no present, and no past,
No essence that his need may not distil,
All pressed into his service, but he knows
Only the immediate care, if that be good;
The little focus that his words enclose;
As the poor joiner, working at his wood,
Knew not the tree from which the planks were taken,
Knew not the glade from which the trunk was brought,

82

Knew not the soil in which the roots were fast,
Nor by what centuries of gales the boughs were shaken,
But holds them all beneath his hands at last.

Crafts-
men

Much goes to little making,—law and skill,
Tradition's usage, each man's separate gift;
Till the slow worker sees that he has wrought
More than he knew of builded truth,
As one who slips through years of youth,
Leaving his young indignant rage,
And finds the years' insensible drift
Brings him achievement with the truce of age.

AUTUMN

AUTUMN

Angelus

How slow the darkness comes, once day-
　　light's gone,
A slowness natural after English day,
So unimpassioned, tardy to move on,
No southern violence that burns away,
Ardent to live, and eager to be done.
The twilight lingers, etching tree on sky;
The gap's a portal on the ridge's crest;
The partridge coveys call beyond the rye;
Still some red bar of sunset cracks the west;
The orange harvest-moon like a dull sun
Rolls silent up the east above the hill;
Earth like a sleeper breathes, and all is still
This hour of after-day, the dying day's bequest,
This autumn dusk, when neither day nor night
Urges a man to strive or sleep; he stands
Filled with the calm of that familiar place,
Idle the shaft beneath his folded hands,
He who must work the lowlands of his farm,
Making tenacity his only creed,
Taking of death and birth his daily need,
Viewing mortality without alarm.

Autumn But brief, but short, this hour of quietude
Gives pause to labour; but a breathing-space
Granted, before necessity renewed
Twists up the sinews of his fortitude;

For now the year draws on towards its ending.
Squirrel has hoarded all his nuts, and man,
(Laying for yet another spring his plan,)
Counts over what he has for winter's spending.
Granary's full with heaped and dusty store:
Apples on attic floor
Throughout the house their brackish smell are
    sending;
The steepled ricks with frost are hoar
In silent yard; the harvest's at its sleeping;
That's slumber now, which once was heyday reaping.
Now retrospect and prospect have their share,
For autumn like the Janus of the year
Holds spring to spring in double-handed keeping.
That sleeps, which once was live; but in the womb
Newly conceived, as corn within the ear,
Another sowing ripens to its bloom.
Further you may not know, but only this:
Nature's an enemy who calls no armistice.
Mistrust the seeming truce, that in the pyre
Of distant woods, and in the gardens' fire,
In pheasants running bronze on furrowed mould,
Burnishes autumn with a coat of gold.

Therefore towards the stubble turn your plough; *Autumn*
Cut gashes new across the healing earth;
Spare not your servant, since to man austere
No respite comes, but bend beneath your vow
Reluctant fields, and bring new life to birth.

Homer and Hesiod and Virgil knew *Plough-*
The ploughshare in its reasonable shape, *ing*
Classical from the moment it was new,
Sprung ready-armed, ordained without escape,
And never bettered though man's cunning grew,
And barbarous countries joined the classic reach:
Coulter and swingletree and share and haft
Frugal of ornament as peasants' speech,
Strong to their use and simple as their craft,
Whether to turn the ridge or cleave the rean.
And as the slow Egyptian turns the dark
Loam in his narrow valley where the green
Draws the rich record of the river's mark,
Or as the Mede across his Asian plain,
Watched by the circling mountains topped with snow,
Scores the poor furrow for his meagre wheat
With wooden yoke and lurching buffalo
Pricked by the lazy goad,
And leaves his sowing to the care of God
And takes the southern road
To summer pastures, where the waters flow,
Driving his train of ponies roughly shod

89

Plough- And camels with grave bells, that surly go
ing Where immemorial caravans have trod,
Marking the trackway with their whitened bones,
His four-span waggons with their homely load,
Black curly lambs that scramble on the stones,
Startling the cricket and the crested lark,
And after summer northward moves again
To reap his harvest in the wickering heat,—
So set your English share, that as a lover tills
The breaking field, and let the blade be keen;
Brace up your hames that collars may not irk,
And urge your horses to the guiding drills,
But knot your hempen reins, and only yerk
Your team by voice, for they will strain
Against a fitful soil, and nobler work
Spared the impatient checking of the rein.
Ploughing's begun among the gentle hills;
Wide skies where cloudy cities travel white
Canopy little acres; in the blanched serene
Tent of the heaven wheel the untidy rooks,
And settle, gawky, on the browning tracks,
While man and horse pursue their ancient rite.

Thresh- Carted away are all the leaning stooks,
ing And from the stackyard comes the thresher's purr.
England's a humming hive till threshing's done
And chaff-motes blowing from the emptied sacks

Mellow the barn in beams of dusty sun.   *Thresh-*
Threshing's a game which sets the farm astir   *ing*
On fine October mornings when the mist
Melts to reveal between the steaming stacks
The thresher lumbering slowly up the lane.
The gang swarms out in jolly morning vein;
Unricker, leather strap about his wrist,
Sackman, and stacker, and the loutish hands,
And dairymaid, agreeable to be kissed,
And farmer's wife, come out to see the fun
After a week of baking loaf and pie,
Admires the young men with a roguish eye;
And barn-door hens that pick among the grain
And terrier nosing round for rats, and bands
Of children, rather shy.
Straw, chaff, and grain, once work's begun,
Clean winnowed, sorted fine,
Heap in appointed place, all rising swift,
And prudent farmer measures out his thrift,
And takes his sacks, and thankful sets them by,
Each fat and solid as a new-killed swine,
Till they may fill his boarded granary.

And other cares in autumn fill the days,   *Hedging*
The care of gardens and of roadside ways.   *and*
The weazen hedger with his hook and stick,   *Ditching*
Brown as a root himself, and stoutly gloved,

Hedging   Brishes the hedges, shaving countryside
and   Like a cropped schoolboy; brambles, and the loved
Ditching Dog-rose, with hazel-shoots and thorny quick
Shrivel to bonfire heaps along the waste
From Michaelmas to Hallowtide
That hedges be more closely interlaced
Without a gap or flaw
Next spring in chequered England, growing thick
Against young stock or colts, for mark the law:
If cattle stray and browse on neighbours' ground,
You may go seek them in the common pound.

Gar-   And gardener, let your spud be sharp to ridge
dener The loam from spiny hedge to hedge;
Labour within your garden square
Till back be broke and light grow rare,
But never heed the sinews' pain
If you may snatch before the rain
Crisp days when clods will turn up rough;
Gentleman robin brown as snuff
With spindle legs and bright round eye
Shall be your autumn company.
Trench deep; dig in the rotting weeds;
Slash down the thistle's greybeard seeds;
Then make the frost your servant; make
His million fingers pry and break
The clods by glittering midnight stealth
Into the necessary tilth.

Then may you shoulder spade and hoe, *Gar-*
And heavy-booted homeward go, *dener*
For no new flowers shall be born
Save hellebore on Christmas morn,
And bare gold jasmine on the wall,
And violets, and soon the small
Blue netted iris, like a cry
Startling the sloth of February.

What of the woodman and his livelihood? *Wood-*
Once in ten years the woodman with his axe *craft*
Felling slim undergrowth from stubby boles,
Shall bare the auburn flooring of the copse,
Its ridges, and the sandy rabbit-holes.
Then shall he pare the twigs, and set in stacks
His tall young ash and stripling chestnut poles
That presently shall serve the wreathing hops,
And he shall peel the bark of shorter wood
Clean as a cat in pattens, smelling good,
And sharpen to a point for stakes and spiles,
The whittled slivers flying as he chops,
And lash the shaven wood in ready piles.

But in late autumn with his ropes and guys
He'll go along the peaty forest-tracks
To seek the nobler prize
Blazed with the timber-master's scarlet mark.

93

Wood-
craft Oak will he fell in spring, to gain the bark,
But ash and elm in winter, and the beech
In the short daylight of November thrown,
By Christmas shall lie open, fair to bleach,
As white and hard as bone.
The smoke coils blue above the little camp;
There, in the clearing at the fourfold wents,
On mould of leaves forgotten, reeking, damp
And heavy with autumnal redolence,
Leviathan lies prone.
Bare as the royal antlers of a stag,
His branches fork, and strive to scorn the ground,
Being born for heaven and by heaven crowned,
But man to dust and trees to timber fall,
And comes the hearse or comes the timber-wain
With nut-brown team, patient to stand or haul,
And like a naked savage bound in chain,
With limbs once proud that now through ordure
      drag,
A captive moves upon his way in thrall;
And that live spirit that once lit the tree,
Fled as a bird when first the ruin came,
Sees only death, defeat, and consequent shame,
Great dignity become a husk; as we
Looking upon the dead demand in vain
Some future use for such mortality;
But being as gods to fallen trees, we know
The lowly uses not within their ken,

94

Re-fashioning their form to live again,   *Wood-*
A humble phoenix stripped of memory.   *craft*

Their past is sure,
Those woods deep-rooted in the swirl of time,
Temples of myth and piety and fear,
Lovely, obscure;
Dark was the ilex in the Grecian vales,
Crooked the olive, murmurous the lime.
No woodsman but had heard the Dryad cry,
No girl but knew the goat-foot faun was nigh,
And saw the satyr through the branches leer,
And fled from those too-peopled solitudes
Into the open fields of maize and rye.
And women still have memories of woods,
Older than any personal memories;
Writhen, primeval roots, though heads be fair,
Like trees that fan the air with delicacies,
With leaves and birds among the upper air,
High, lifted canopies,
Green and black fingers of the trees, dividing
And reaching out towards an otherwhere,
Threaded with birds and birds' sweet sudden gliding,
Pattern and jargoning of tree-tops, such a world
Tangled and resonant and earth-deriding,
Now with the rain-drops' rounded globes bepearled,
And little sullen moons of mistletoe,
Now fretted with the sun, when foxes play

Wood-
craft   At fables on the dun and foxlike ground
Between the tree-trunks, and the squirrels go
Scuttering with a beechnut newly found,
To vex the pigeon and to scare the jay.

Of such a tall and airy world are they,
Women and woods, with shadowed aisles profound
That none explore.
—Birches, frail whispering company, are these?
Or lovely women rooted into trees?
Daughters of Norsemen, on a foreign shore
Left hostage, while the galley draws away,
Beating its rise and fall on manifold oar,
Beating a pathway to the broken coasts,
Forgetful of its ghosts?

There is a kinship: down the open ride
She strays, eternal nymph, and glances swift
Into the ambushed depths on either side;
Now fears the shadows, now the rift,
Now fears the silence, now the rustling leaf
That like a footfall with a nearing stride
Startles the stronghold of her unbelief.
Woods are her enemies, yet once she went
Fleeing before a god, and, all but spent,
Slipped from his arms, herself become a tree.
She has forgotten; wood's an enemy;
She has no knowledge of the woodland tracks,

Only a knowledge of her jeopardy, *Wood-*
And with lost steps, neglectful of her pride, *craft*
Stumbles towards the music of the axe.
There, brown old sylvan god, the woodsman plies
His craft and drives his wedge,
Spitting to ease the rub of tool on hands,
And she arrested at the clearing's edge
Awakened stands,
With panic terror fading from her eyes.

Now I have told the year from dawn to dusk, *Autumn*
Its morning and its evening and its noon;
Once round the sun our slanting orbit rolled,
Four times the seasons changed, thirteen the
    moon;
Corn grew from seed to husk,
The young spring grass to provender for herds;
Drought came, and earth was grateful for the rain;
The bees streamed in and out the summer hives;
Birds wildly sang; were silent; birds
With summer's passing fitfully sang again;
The loaded waggon crossed the field; the sea
Spread her great generous pasture as a robe
Whereon the slow ships, circling statelily,
Are patterned round the globe.
The ample busyness of life went by,
All the full busyness of lives

97

Autumn Unknown to fame, made lovely by no words:
The shepherd lonely in the winter fold;
The tiller following the eternal plough
Beneath a stormy or a gentle sky;
The sower with his gesture like a gift
Walking the furrowed hill from base to brow;
The reaper in the piety of thrift
Binding the sheaf against his slanted thigh.

Or- And lastly,—since it was of Kent I told,
chards Kent, and the parcels of her acreage,—
Peculiar autumn crops
Leave one thing more to tell,
Spilt from the horn of plenty to my page,
Spicing my line with tart or resinous smell.
Apples and hops make Kent's clean autumn wine,
Orchard and garden, loaded, looped with swags,
Scarlet and green, on bough and bine;
Heavy as apples, say we, light as hops,
Where the leafy awning sags,
And weighted boughs are crutched on forkèd props.

I told in spring of the orchard's enemies,
Wrapped in cocoon or pert upon the wing,
And of the care that prudent growers bring,
But now the swoln fulfilment of the trees,
Coloured and round,
Demands another order: nimble boys,

Reared ladders, bushel baskets on the ground, *Or-*
And pick, pick, pick, while days are calm and fine. *chards*
These orchards that have lonely stood since spring,
Swelling their fruit unnoted in the sun,
Are populous suddenly, with ringing voice,
September mornings, when the sun's yet low,
And dew upon the leas
Makes brambles glisten and the mushrooms grow.
Codlin's already stripped; his day was done
When August holidays were first begun,
Being the children's apple, earliest ripe
And nothing worth for keeping; only worth
Young teeth, and summer fun.
But Quarrendens, and Russets nicely browned,
And common Councillors, of varied stripe,
And Pippins smelling of the rainy earth
Wait to be harvested
With Peasgood Nonesuch, giant in his girth,
Cox, Blenheim, Ribstone, properly renowned,
Apples that wait for Christmas, darkly stored
On shelf or floor, not touching, one by one.
But by the red cheek never be misled;
For virtue, flavour, seek the acid green,
Of looks less kindly, but of sharp reward
Like stringent wit that keeps a matter keen.

Full carts, full baskets, in the misty sun,
And cider claims the windfall on the sward.

Making
Cider

I saw within the wheelwright's shed
The big round cartwheels, blue and red;
A plough with blunted share;
A blue tin jug; a broken chair;
And paint in trial patchwork square
Slapped up against the wall;
The lumber of the wheelwright's trade,
And tools on benches neatly laid,
The brace, the adze, the awl;

And, framed within the latticed panes,
Above the cluttered sill,
Saw rooks upon the stubble hill
Seeking forgotten grains;

And all the air was sweet and shrill
With juice of apples heaped in skips,
Fermenting, rotten, soft with bruise,
And all the yard was strewn with pips,
Discarded pulp, and wrung-out ooze
That ducks with rummaging flat bill
Searched through beside the cider-press
To gobble in their greediness.

The young men strained upon the crank
To wring the last reluctant inch.
They laughed together, fair and frank,
And threw their loins across the winch.

A holiday from field and dung,
From plough and harrow, scythe and spade,
To dabble in another trade,
To crush the pippins in the slats,
And see that in the little vats
An extra pint was wrung;
While round about the worthies stood,
Profuse in comment, praise or blame,
Content the press should be of wood,
Advising rum, decrying wheat,
And black strong sugar makes it sweet,
But still resolved, with maundering tongue,
That cider could not be the same
As once when they were young;
But still the young contemptuous men
Laughed kindly at their old conceit,
And strained upon the crank again.

Now barrels ranged in portly line
Mature through winter's sleep,
Aping the leisured sloth of wine
That dreams by Tiber or by Rhine,
Mellowing slow and deep;
But keen and cold the northern nights
Sharpen the quiet yard,
And sharp like no rich southern wine
The tang of cider bites;
For here the splintered stars and hard

Making
Cider

Making *Hold England in a frosty guard,*
Cider *Orion and the Pleiades*
    Above the wheelwright's shed,
    And Sirius resting on the trees
    While all the village snores abed.

Hop Hops ripen to their picking. Down the rows
Garden Of pickers by their tally-baskets bent,
  The gaitered master goes,
  Slapping his leggings with a hazel switch,
  Nodding good-day to folk he knows,
  From London slums poured yearly into Kent,
  Waking the province with their cockney slang,
  And feathered hats, and fear of showers;
  Down leafy tunnels, dappled by the sun,
  Down sea-green aisles, where loam is brown and rich
  Between the hills, and overhead the flowers
  In pale imponderable clusters hang,
  He loiters, followed by his spaniel bitch
  Close in to heel, sulky for lack of gun.
  Passed from his keeping now, those bines
  That since their earliest shooting had his care;
  Already severed, half the lines
  Are fallen withered, and the poles are bare,
  But in the tallies rise the soft green heaps,
  High, and are emptied, once again to fill,
  For carts between the garden and the kiln

Slow but unceasing ply,   *Hop*
And down the trampled lane come for a fresh   *Garden*
    supply.

Dusk sends the pickers home to camp,   *Oast*
But the country works while London sleeps.
Within the oast the sulphurous furnace roars;
Men shovel coal, and clang the doors,
And in an inner room play cards and dice
Beneath a smoking lamp;
Swear; spit; and grumble at the crop, the price,
The master's profit and the labourer's wage
With a fictitious indignation; rage
Born of sound understanding, sprung
Like lovers' quarrels from a prickly tongue,
Vain of its independence and its wit,
With hearts belying speech,
Each against foreigner defending each,
But bitter among friends,—unspoken laws.
Comes here the master: silence falls.
Shadows of men on whitewashed walls
Throw dice; deal cards; turn down the lamp; puff
    smoke;
Rise up; and on a sudden redly lit
Pass to the kiln like demons; fiercely stoke;
And to the inner room return to swear and spit,
To gamble and to grumble, spit and swear.

Oast   But he, the master, climbs the ladder-stair
To the upper loft, where silence and pale peace
Hold volatile lease;
The upper loft, where mountains on the floor
Of sapless flowers, sap-robbed flowers, swell
Bulky and weightless, ashen as fair hair
Beneath a lamp, ashen as moonlit corn,
As stubble newly shorn,
Hops dried and ready for the rhythmic press
Crushing their levity to a nothingness
Of prosy tonnage scribbled on a slate,
—Those airy mountains packed in terms of weight;—
The press that whirls its shadow on the bare
White wall and raftered ceiling, wheel and spoke
Distorted, laying like a heavier cloak
Burdens of resin on the loaded air.

Now the old drier shuffles across the loft,
Opens the oast-house door,
Where hops spread drying, sappy, green, and soft,
Wreathed with the mounting of the faint blue smoke
In a round chamber with a pointed roof,
And the scent overpowers.
Knee-deep he slouches, kicking up the flowers;
Like an old priest at some clandestine rite
Round the white walls, he, dressed in white,
Stealthily travels, ancient and aloof.
Ancient as man on earth, man turns to wine

Or bread earth's produce; seeks escape or need;   *Oast*
Release, necessity, the alternating creed;
Necessity, release; food, anodyne.
So the old drier, forty or fifty years,
Kicks up the hops, that they be evenly dried
Each autumn as the harvest comes again,
Grown old at a lonely task; he hears
The sound of voices in the yard outside,
The clang of furnace doors, the tread of men;
And they, as they swing homeward down the lane,
Look back at the oast and the single lighted pane
Like a square beacon yellow in the night,
And know that the drier slouches round the wall.

Yet I recall   *Vintage*
Another harvest, not beneath this sky
So Saxon-fair, so washed by dews and rain;
Another harvest, where the gods still rouse,
And stretch, and waken with the evenfall.
Down from the hill the slow white oxen crawl,
Dragging the purple waggon heaped with must,
Raising on sundered hoofs small puffs of dust,
With scarlet tassels on their milky brows,
Gentle as evening moths. Beneath the yoke
Lounging against the shaft they fitful strain
To draw the waggon on its creaking spoke,
And all the vineyard folk
With staves and shouldered tools surround the wain.

Vintage The wooden shovels take the purple stain,
　　　　　The dusk is heavy with the wine's warm load;
　　　　　Here the long sense of classic measure cures
　　　　　The spirit weary of its difficult pain;
　　　　　Here the old Bacchic piety endures,
　　　　　Here the sweet legends of the world remain.
　　　　　Homeric waggons lumbering the road;
　　　　　Virgilian litanies among the bine;
　　　　　Pastoral sloth of flocks beneath the pine;
　　　　　Under the chestnut trees the rootling swine,
　　　　　The swineherd watching, propped upon his goad.
　　　　　Who could so stand, and see this evening fall,
　　　　　This calm of husbandry, this redolent tilth,
　　　　　This terracing of hills, this vintage wealth,
　　　　　Without the pagan sanity of blood
　　　　　Mounting his veins in young and tempered health?
　　　　　Who could so stand, and watch processional
　　　　　The vintners, herds, and flocks in dusty train
　　　　　Wend through the molten evening to regain
　　　　　The terraced farm and trodden threshing-floor
　　　　　Where late the flail
　　　　　That tossed the maize in scud of gritty ore,
　　　　　Now lies half-buried in the heap of grain,—
　　　　　Who could so watch, and not forget the rack
　　　　　Of wills worn thin and thought become too frail,
　　　　　Nor roll the centuries back
　　　　　And feel the sinews of his soul grow hale,
　　　　　Knowing himself for Rome's inheritor?

AUTUMN

O Mantuan! that sang the bees and vines,
The tillage and the flocks,
I saw the round moon rise above the pines,
One quiet planet prick the greening west,
As goats came leaping up the stony crest
And the crook'd goatherd moved between the rocks.
That moon, that star, above my English Weald,
Hung at that hour, and I not there to see;
Shining through mist above the dew-drenched field,
Making a cavern of the plumy tree.
Then all my deep acquaintance with that land,
Crying for words, welled up; as Man who knows
That Nature, tender enemy, harsh friend,
Takes from him soon the little that she gave,
Yet for his span will labour to defend
His courage, that his soul be not a slave,
Whether on waxen tablet or on loam,
Whether with stylus or with share and heft
The record of his passage he engrave,
And still, in toil, takes heart to love the rose.

Then thought I, Virgil! how from Mantua reft,
Shy as a peasant in the courts of Rome,
You took the waxen tablets in your hand,
And out of anger cut calm tales of home.

Ispahan, April 1926.